HOW TO
DESTROY THE WORLD

AN AUTHOR'S GUIDE TO WRITING
DYSTOPIA AND POST-APOCALYPSE

A TREVENA

How to Destroy the World is also available as an ebook Guidebook.

The content of the ebook is the same. It offers a more portable version of this workbook, and simply requires you to provide your own space for notes.

AUTHOR GUIDES SERIES

30 DAYS OF WORLDBUILDING
An Author's Step-by-Step Guide to Building Fictional Worlds

HOW TO DESTROY THE WORLD
An Author's Guide to Writing Dystopia and Post-Apocalypse

FROM SANCTITY TO SORCERY
An Author's Guide to Building Belief Structures and Magic Systems

HOW TO CREATE HISTORY
An Author's Guide to Creating History, Myths, and Monsters

COMPLETE WORLDBUILDING
An Author's Step-by-Step Guide to Building Fictional Worlds

angelinetrevena.co.uk/worldbuilding

CONTENTS

INTRODUCTION

I am one of those authors who have been writing, pretty much, since they were old enough to hold a pen. I have a folder of old stories, typed up on an old typewriter, that I don't even remember having written.

I was rarely seen without a book in my hand, and spent every spare hour I had, buried deep in fantastical worlds. I was lucky in that my parents encouraged it. They never told me that I was wasting my time, or to keep my head out of the clouds. They even let me read at the dinner table, eating one-handed.

I was also lucky to have access to a local library, and quickly worked my way through the fantasy catalogue in their children's section. I swept my way through all of the Choose Your Own Adventure books; not only following the adventures of kids— passing into a fantasy world to fight dragons, mounted on their bicycle steeds—but I got to control the stories. I could re-read them over and over, choosing different paths each time, creating a multitude of adventures for myself.

My love of speculative fiction had started young. It was my dad's job to read the bedtime stories each night, all of us huddled together to listen. He often picked books from his own collection which, almost exclusively, consisted of classic sci-fi novels. And so, as a child, my bedtime stories were written by the likes of H.G. Wells and John Wyndham. Looking back, I suspect that *The War of the Worlds* and *The Day of the Triffids* were probably inappropriate choices for children about to go to sleep, but it must have caught my imagination. I will forever thank my dad for introducing me to such tales.

I was first introduced to dystopia in my late teens, when we read Margaret Atwood's *The Handmaid's Tale* as part of our English Literature A-Level course. It was my first Atwood book, and it fuelled a continuing love of her words. It was also my first taste of what would come to be, not just my favourite genre to read, but also my favourite to write.

Alongside my English Literature A-Level, my other two subjects were Theatre Studies and Sociology. Learning about the work of Karl Marx, I became very interested in Marxism, seeing the value in his words and beliefs when applied to a modern society. I felt, within the scope of my limited life experience, that my eyes had been opened. Of course, the opening of our eyes is a lifelong process that will never be fully completed. But this part of my education was something of a revelation.

I grew up in poverty. I was a statistic. And, for the first time, I was seeing the relevance of this within society as a whole, rather than from the perspective of my own, personal, experience of it. I am also female, and that became more important, and more relevant in a wider capacity. I was seeing the world afresh, and viewing myself as a product of it, and a part in it. A player in the wider game of life.

Everyone tells you that, when you have children, you see the world anew, through your child's eyes. Eyes of wonder, where everything is magic. As a parent of two, I can tell you that this is absolutely true. You do rediscover a wonder in the smallest of things that you have long-since given up noticing at all. But there are many moments of similar unveiling-of-the-new in our adult lives. Sadly, they tend to be based more on becoming more cynical, or hardened, or cautious. They may not be bathed in the dizzy glow of childhood, but they are equally important, and transformative. They are still massive shifts in our understanding of the world, and ourselves, and deserve recognition.

We learn through doing, just as babies do, and, most of all, we learn through falling.

My fiction is an interpretation of my world view. My world view is an interpretation of everything that has influenced and pressed upon me in my life. My culture and its history, my peers, my parents, my personal experiences, both good and bad. It is also an interpretation of trying to step inside 'the other', and to see the world from another perspective.

At university I studied Drama and Creative Writing, and wandered away from my love of magic and fantastical worlds. I can't say why, it just happened. Perhaps I felt pressure to finally grow up. Perhaps I felt the oncoming cynicism of adulthood. Perhaps my university course pushed me towards literary fiction. Perhaps I simply needed a break from it for a while. I don't know.

After university, as I began to navigate the confusing and cynical world of adulthood, I barely read anything at all. For a long time, I hardly managed a handful of books a year. During this time, I read my first ever Stephen King book. It was, interestingly enough, *On Writing* that I picked up first, and I finished it in just a few days. And so, I was brought back to literature with a renewed desire to read, as well as to write.

Although I've been writing since I was very young, it was never my ambition to make a career from it. I wanted to act. I wanted to be on stage. My whole childhood was filled with drama lessons, singing lessons, lessons in several different forms of dance. I was always performing; music concerts, amateur dramatics, school plays. If there was a spotlight, I was in it.

While I was at university, studying Drama, I discovered that I wasn't enjoying it as much as I'd expected to. I had a long heart-to-heart with myself, finally accepting that the ambition I'd had all of my life, my singular goal, simply wasn't what I wanted anymore. And it was difficult to let go of. This vision had shaped my entire life, my entire personality, and I had nothing to replace it with.

But, I couldn't pretend to myself anymore. And, as I continued with my degree, I came to the conclusion that I didn't want to be onstage, blinking into the spotlight, speaking someone else's words. What I wanted was to sit in the back of a darkened auditorium, watching other people perform my words. I wanted to write.

Even with this revelation, I still didn't imagine myself making writing into any kind of a career. The first Kindle wouldn't come on the market for another six years. The publishing landscape was a very different one to what it is today. Becoming a published author was a pipe-dream. One that seemed to rely far more on luck than any kind of talent. A who-you-know rather than a what-you-know industry. And for a young woman barely into her twenties, and still reeling from losing the footing of the one constant she'd had in her life, it all seemed like an impossibility.

As part of my Creative Writing class, our tutor asked us to write a personal introduction to an imaginary book about ourselves. Much like this introduction you're reading right now. The difference being, in that imagined introduction, I wrote "I can't imagine writing ever being anything more than a hobby for me." When I wrote that, I wouldn't have believed I'd ever be writing one for real.

When our assignments were returned, my tutor had highlighted that sentence, responding with the note "That would be a shame." That single comment began a shift in mindset which, over the following years, led me to this moment right now. And this book, through all those that have come before it.

Inspiration tends to come from the most unexpected sources, at the most unexpected of moments.

And I'm sure that my tutor has no idea of the impact she had. Of the wheels she set into motion. Of the future she helped to craft. She dropped a small pebble into a pool, and its ripples are still radiating outwards.

USING THIS WORKBOOK

If you're looking to write dystopian or post-apocalyptic fiction for the first time, and you're not sure where to start, this is the book for you. If you'd like to deepen and expand your idea for a dystopian, destroyed world, this is the book for you. If you find the idea of these genres daunting, and you've been putting off starting to write, this is definitely the book for you.

This workbook breaks the genres down, exploring the worldbuilding and ideas behind them. It will lead you through the process of creating a strong, solid basis for your world, characters, and story. It will help you to understand your readers' expectations, as well as showing you how those expectations can be twisted, upended, and smashed.

This book and its prompts are not, by any means, exhaustive. Depending on your story, your characters, and the world you need to create for them, you may need to continue worldbuilding beyond the scope of this workbook. Likewise, not all of this book will necessarily be relevant to your specific story.

Think of it like a garden. This book gives you the foundation to build upon. It helps you to plant the seeds, and offers you seeds you may not have considered planting yourself. But, you'll need to cultivate it, and water it. And, you may have plants of your own that you want to include. A special tree, your favourite flower. You may like to have a pond, or a bench, or a marquee.

The other thing this workbook offers is a safe, singular place to keep all of your notes. I hereby give you permission to write in this book. To write in every gap you can find. To doodle, and scribble, and squeeze ideas into the margins. When you come to writing your story, keep this book next to you, so that all the things you need to know about your story are in easy reach.

I have purposefully left the work pages of this book as blank as possible, because we all like to work in different ways. Draw pictures, create tables and graphs, or fill it with neatly written notes. Use it in the way that works best for you.

Above all, enjoy creating your dystopian or post-apocalyptic world. Enjoy exploring it, and watching it come to life around you. I promise; even if you're building the darkest of worlds, the most terrifying of futures, you'll enjoy it. Even if only in a malicious, vengeful God-like kind of way!

As a simple human, this may be the closest you'll come to performing real magic. To visualise an entire world from nothing. To pluck things from the air and make them real. To take breath on the wind and form it into something tangible. That is the most real, purest magic I know of.

Of course, I'm being presumptuous here. You may have magical abilities beyond my comprehension. In fact, you may even be a little more than human...

PREPARING TO DESTROY THE WORLD

Dystopia and post-apocalypse are, strictly speaking, sub-genres of science fiction.

If that sends a cold shard of fear through your heart, and results in you running around declaring loudly "But I'm not a sci-fi author, I don't know anything about science", fear not. I know exactly how you feel. Because I did the same thing.

I know next to nothing about space travel, or how astronauts go to the toilet, or how hyper-drive warp speed boost initiators work. In fact, I'm pretty much clueless as to how my toaster toasts, or my kettle kettles. Electricity is a little bit like magic, and self checkouts are something that should have remained in the realms of science fiction.

And, if you're anything like me, that's absolutely fine. Don't stress.

As an author, as a human being, there is one thing that you do know. And you know it well. And that is: people. You know how to person. (At least, to some degree, and only after coffee.)

First and foremost, before anything else, writing dystopian and post-apocalyptic fiction is about writing people. It's about writing characters. As, of course, almost any kind of fiction is.

Absolutely everything in your story and your worldbuilding should always come back to character. They are the reason your readers stick with the story. They are the reason your readers keep turning the pages. They are the reason your readers fall in love with your book. You can write the most fantastic, amazing, perfect story of all time, but without characters that your readers can believe in, can root for, you have nothing.

Don't stress because you were never very good at physics or chemistry, don't worry if you don't know the mass of each planet in the solar system or, in fact, if you can't even name them all. As long as you know how to write people, you can write wonderfully dystopian worlds, and fantastic post-apocalyptic worlds for them to exist in. To survive in. To change and revolutionise.

Because, while these genres are, officially, under the metallic, robotic umbrella of science fiction, they don't need to be heavy on the science. They don't need to involve space travel, or futuristic technology, or clever survival strategies. All they need is compelling characters.

You can build a world that is far more based in fantasy than it is in sci-fi. You can build a world in which technology has actually regressed, or been destroyed, or outlawed. You can build a world that is, clearly, a future vision of earth, or something that is barely recognisable as the same place. You can set your world three hundred years into an unknown future, or you can set it tomorrow.

So, don't worry about filling your world with scientific, technological, medical, and survivalist knowledge you don't have. It doesn't need it. It's your future vision, and you can create it however you like. After all, the only person who can tell you, with absolute certainty, that your future vision is wrong, is a time-traveller. And, generally, there don't tend to be very many of those. (Besides, I hear they're usually more into romance novels.)

If you need it, here it is. This is your official permission to write whatever the hell you like. Whatever excites you, and sets your soul ablaze. It doesn't matter if it's crazy, outlandish, or entirely unlikely. If you do your job properly, with the characters and the world you create for them, then you can get your readers to accept almost anything.

Go mad. Make your dream a reality. If you want to, you can always reign it back in later. If you want.

The other permission I give you now, is the permission to be truly, deeply, and unapologetically evil. Pull up every malicious thought you have ever had, every moment of rage, every hardened ball of guilt, or jealousy. Relight that fire of hatred that you extinguished after you left school. All of that, take it, smoosh it into a malformed lump of play dough, with all the colours mixed together. Remember not to taste it. Even out of curiosity.

That lump of grossness is what you will use to build your world. Have fun. It's meant to be fun. In fact, practice your booming evil laugh. Right now. Give it a go. There, doesn't that feel good?

This is the place to pour all of that evil. To express the sadistic side of you. Put it all here, and don't forget that evil laugh. It's ok, you can work on it. If you keep all the evil here, then you can go about your real life with a lovely, sunny personality, and stroke kittens and puppies, and ride around on rainbows. Because life is all about balance, right?

Next time you see someone with a beaming smile, ask yourself what book they might be writing at home...

WORLDBUILDING BASICS

Now that you are, officially, a science fiction writer, we need to discuss worldbuilding.

You will be creating a world for your characters. It may be very, very similar to the one you're living in right now, but with some fictional additions. Perhaps an alien invasion, or an uprising of the animals, or a plague of killer vegetables. I don't know, it's your world.

On the other hand, you may be creating a barren wasteland of a world, with people living underground, and trying to survive after the complete collapse of civilisation.

The amount of worldbuilding you're going to do, depends very much on the story that you want to write. There's no shame in starting small, with very few changes, and working your way up to projecting your characters far into a post-apocalyptic future. Start wherever you feel comfortable. Or not. If you're the kind of person that likes a challenge, then go for it.

Worldbuilding doesn't need to be difficult, or complicated. It doesn't need to take forever, or be an excuse for never actually writing the book. It doesn't need to be overwhelming or intimidating. At the other end of the scale, it shouldn't be something that you haphazardly bolt on in a last-minute panic.

Your worldbuilding should be tightly integrated with your plot and your characters. Your characters, and their goals, their struggles, their journey, that is the reason your readers show up. That's the reason they keep reading. I will never stop banging on about this, because it is important. You can have the most amazing world, but if you don't populate it with compelling, sympathetic, and relatable characters, readers will simply stop turning the pages. Likewise, if you write amazing characters, and put them into a flat, paper world, your readers won't want to walk along with them, or explore with them.

Just as you want your readers to believe in your characters, you want them to believe in your world, too.

Let them smell the salt on the breeze, hear the buzzing of the insects. Let them feel the heat of the burning buildings, and suffer the oppression of the government. Let them walk every single step with your characters. Invite them in. And invite them to stay. Whether they want to set up home there, or fight to change it.

Your worldbuilding is equally as important as your story and characters. Give your characters somewhere real to live, and give your readers somewhere real to visit. You simply can't separate these things out if you want to write the best book that you can.

There are a few different ways to approach worldbuilding, and which you choose, will depend on your goals and your story.

DIFFERENT TYPES OF WORLDBUILDING

Building a whole new fictional world:
This method involves creating an entirely fictional world from scratch. Somewhere that does not, and never has, existed. It may have similarities to our world, and it may have huge differences. Think along the lines of second-world fantasies penned by the likes of J.R.R. Tolkien or C.S. Lewis. You may well choose this option if your book is going to be more on the fantasy side. There's no reason why you can't write a dystopian urban fantasy, or a post-apocalyptic epic fantasy.

A real place with a parallel fictional world:
The other way is to set your story in a real place, and have a fictional world created alongside it, usually invisible or hidden from the general public. Such as in Neil Gaiman's Neverwhere, or Harry Potter, or Hellboy. The fictional side of the world may be tightly integrated with the real world, or it may be quite separate. This would depend, again, on your story.

A real place with an alternative past or future:
This may be taking a real existing place, London, for example, and giving it an alternative or altered history. Imagine if the Great Fire of London had actually been started by dragons. How would that change the world today? Or it may be taking the real-world place, and throwing it into your imagined future. This is very common in dystopian and post-apocalyptic genres, and is your most likely choice.

When using this style of worldbuilding, your map is usually, largely, already done for you. There is likely to be some changes, such as missing landmarks, or different names for places. The extent of the changes would entirely depend on your story, and how different you have imagined the past or future of this place.

Whichever kind of world you're building, your objective is still the same: to create a believable world that your readers can really imagine walking around in.

THE HISTORY OF YOUR WORLD

Your current world is a product of everything that ever happened there, and in a dystopian or post-apocalyptic world, this is particularly important.

First lets talk about the apocalypse. It may well be that your story is set so far into the future, that there's no one left alive who actually remembers the apocalyptic event. Or life from before it. That doesn't mean that it hasn't left its mark. Its scars.

People may have retreated underground to escape a poisonous atmosphere, or a blazing, burning sun. People may have evolved, or adapted to the new state of the world. The set-up of society may have changed because of the event. Or people might be fearful of the specific cause of it. You might be writing about life after a robot uprising, or a plague, or the awakening of dragons.

Alternatively, you may have an older generation who lived through the apocalypse, and a younger generation who have no memory of it. How do those two generations view one another? How do the older generation feel about the world as it is now? Perhaps the past is a goal for society to return to, or a pleasant bit of nostalgia. Maybe it's illegal to talk of the time before with harsh punishments for those who do.

Maybe you're planning on bringing your readers into the action, and making them live through the apocalypse itself.

And when you think about dystopian societies, think about how those changes happened. And how long they took to happen. A singular event may have set society off on a totally different course, or it may have happened gradually, with changes to political or religious opinions over several generations.

Think about the people who pushed back. The ones who could foresee the future. And think about those who simply watched it happen, detached, because it didn't directly affect them. Think about the policy makers, and those making the changes. Think about their reasons for doing it. And think about those washed along on the tide of change. Unable to turn it around. Helpless and drowning.

Once again, you may have people who remember life before, which gives you a wonderfully polarised lens with which to explore the issues in your dystopian world. The inequality. The unfairness. The oppression.

The most important thing that you need to remember is that every time you change something, it affects everything else.

Think about the butterfly effect, and the ripples you might be sending out.

Imagine your world as a pool. Every event, ever construct, every thing you change or create, is like dropping a pebble into the water. Sometimes, the ripples last a few minutes. Sometimes, a few years. Spreading wider. Affecting more people. Sometimes, those ripples last for centuries.

HOW YOUR WORLD AFFECTS CHARACTER AND STORY

You can also use your worldbuilding to create conflict. Remember that conflict is created when your protagonist's goal is interrupted, or opposed, and you can use your world to do that.

Perhaps the most obvious example is if the protagonist's goal requires them to break the law. But you can use other things too: limitations of transport, social norms and expectations, gender roles. The landscape itself can become a physical barrier, or the weather, or a lack of resources. Dystopian and post-apocalyptic worlds offer so much opportunity for this. (It's time to try that evil laugh again.)

And you can use all of this in your worldbuilding to raise the stakes. To increase the tension.

Because your world doesn't exist separately from the people who live in it, and you should create it with those people in mind. They will have opinions about everything. Beliefs, hopes, grievances. Things they love, things they hate. Things they want to change. Things they fight to change.

And these things will differ based on all of their nuances: gender, age, class, religion, etc. So their opinions will be different to the person stood next to them. They may even directly oppose one another. Conflict.

You have to remember that everything comes back to character. You have to remember that you aren't writing a story about a world that happens to have people living in it. You are writing a story about people who happen to live in a particular world.

Worldbuilding. Story. Character. None of these is independent from the others.

THE DIFFERENCE BETWEEN TROPES AND CLICHÉS

There's a lot of pressure to be original in your writing. To be the first person to think of an idea, or a story. To think of a character, or a world for them. Let me say this: originality is overrated.

I've seen lots of writers stressing out because they've come across a book that, from the blurb, sounds like it might be quite similar to what they're writing. I've seen writers almost abandoning their books because of it.

There will always be books with ideas similar to yours. With characters similar to yours. With themes, settings, story elements similar to yours. But, and I can promise you this, there will never, ever be a book exactly like yours.

Why can I be so sure? Because you are unique. You are a product of everything that has ever happened to you. You're a product of your culture, your upbringing, your experiences; both moments of joy and moments of pain. You are a product of every influence that has ever impressed itself upon you: friends, relatives, teachers. Music, movies, books. Beautiful views, shocking news stories, and every thought that has ever crossed your busy mind. There is no other single person on this planet that has had the exact same experience of life as you have, in the exact same doses, at the exact same points.

All of this has created your view of the world. It has moulded your vision of it. And your view of the world, your position in it, is entirely, utterly, and irrevocably unique to you. Just as the world has created you, you will create your world. Unique to you. No one can say what you want to say exactly how you would say it. Because they're standing over there, and their view is totally different to yours.

So don't worry about making your story entirely unique. Don't worry about finding a situation and circumstance that no one, in the history of the world, has ever written about before. The likelihood is, that you won't be able to. It is far more important to focus on telling your story your way. That is what is original. That is what makes it special. The *way* in which you tell the story.

In fact, if you come across other books that are similar to yours, especially if they are popular books, written by a world-famous author, then rejoice. Because there is already a market for your book, and you already know exactly who to market it to.

And so, let's move on to the difference between tropes and clichés.

I'm sure you'll know that a cliché is an overused, trite, stereotyped phrase or idea which has lost its impact, ingenuity, and originality through excessive use over time. Clichés are something to be avoided in literature. They are something that invite eye-rolls from your readers. They have also been known to cause heavy sighing, groans, bad reviews, and, in the worst cases, an incurable impulse to stop reading.

Clichés are viewed, by readers, editors, publishers, and other authors, as a dirty, shameful thing. Something whispered about around corners, or poked at, laughed at. They can kill a book entirely.

Now, I am fully aware that, just a few paragraphs ago, I made the bold statement that 'originality is overrated'. And, I'm also aware that, if taken out of context, it can appear that I am now contradicting myself. That's another thing that will induce tut-tutting and head shaking.

In my defence, here comes some more context for you.

People often toss clichés and tropes into a singular box, shake it up, and mix them together without any care. They seem to think that they are exactly the same thing. And that they are both things to stay clear of. It's a little bit like assuming that all bacteria is bad, and out to kill you. As we know from all of those odd yoghurty-type-but-not-quite-yoghurt drink adverts; there is 'good' bacteria and 'bad' bacteria. To be fair, I don't know any bacteria well enough to make my own decision on which is which. I'll just accept that the authoritative voice-over on such advertisements is not leading me astray.

Let's make this clear: tropes and clichés are very different things, and should be treated as such. However (it's never simple, is it?), there is cross-over, and the line between them is a little shaky and blurry in places.

First, let's define what a trope is. For the sake of context (again), we're going to ignore the literal, dictionary definition of a trope, and apply it more widely in the way that it applies here.

Genre tropes are common and recurring elements of story, attributed to specific genres. For example, the elderly mentor or the chosen one in epic fantasy. The possessed doll or the abandoned asylum in horror. The one true love or the roll in the hay in romance.

Some tropes border on horrible clichés, and some tropes will be so overused that they will become clichés. Condemned to the mercy of the red editing pen.

Other tropes are much loved and enjoyed by readers. There are many, many readers who specifically seek out books containing certain tropes because they enjoy reading them so much.

Now, of course, you can't please everyone. For every reader that loves a particular trope, there will be another who hates it, and avoids all books containing it. That's fine. You cannot please everyone. Let me repeat that, because it's important: you cannot please everyone. If you have an idea that you can write a book that is universally and comprehensively adored by everyone, get it out of your head right now.

Think of tropes as genre markers. As milestones along a route. You don't need to pass every single one of them, and you can meander off that main route any time you wish. In fact, you might like to borrow a milestone marker from another genre route. You might like to mix them together. Or break them apart, and create some kind of mosaic from them.

There may be tropes that can bring your book down. That can risk making it formulaic and predictable. But, at the end of the day, it is your job, as the author, to take a trope and do something new with it. To twist it, and play with it, and paint it a new colour.

So, don't think of tropes as being the same a clichés. They are genre markers that many readers look out for. They're little breadcrumbs, or promises to the reader that they will be reading a book they already know they'll enjoy.

Use the space below to make a note of some story tropes that you enjoy reading. Because, if you enjoy reading them, the chances are that you'll enjoy writing them too.

POPULAR DYSTOPIAN TROPES

Despite the growing popularity of the dystopian genre in recent years, it isn't a modern concept. The word's usage is traced back to a mid-1800s speech addressed to the British government. Although its roots lead back as much as 100 years before that, be it with a slightly different spelling. In fact, the word 'utopia' was first coined in the early 1500s.

There are various theories about whether dystopia sells better in times of social and political upheaval, or in times of calm and peace. But I say that dystopia is for life, not just for Christmas.

Of course, the popularity of particular elements, themes, and tropes changes over time, and changes back, and waxes and wanes. If you think back over the past generations, and track the kinds of dystopias portrayed, you'll find clusters of similarities. Surveillance, out-of-control robots, disease, nuclear war. I'll go more into depth about this in the chapter Following Fear Trends.

Here are some of the popular dystopian tropes. You'll recognise many of them, and you'll be able to apply them to the dystopian books, movies, and TV shows that you know. This list is by no means completely exhaustive, or static. It will keep changing, but this will give you an idea of the kind of story elements you can use to hit those genre markers for your readers.

Many of the tropes here can also be applied to the post-apocalyptic genre. There's a lot of cross-over between the two.

You shouldn't be looking to include all of them, or attempt to shoehorn them, forcibly, into a story they don't fit in. If something in this list sparks off a great story idea, run with it. Or if you see a trope that you really enjoy, use it. And if one gets your head buzzing with a new way of interpreting it, then that's awesome. This list is just a guide. You can choose none of them, or, indeed, use it as a list of things to avoid. It's your book, and there's no right or wrong answer.

I've said it before, and I'll say it again: write the story that makes your soul feel alive.

A Childless Future. For some reason, people just aren't reproducing anymore. And, without children, there's no hope for the future.

It's a Man's World. It sucks to be a woman here.

It's a Woman's World. It sucks to be a man here.

Eat or Be Eaten. Everyone here is toughened, and entirely capable of taking down a tiger with little more than a plastic spoon and a piece of string.

Sadism Rules. Everyone here is either an abuser, or is abused, and no one seems to care.

In the Slums. A story set in the poor part of town.

Where Did Everyone Go? For some reason, the population of the world has been greatly reduced.

For the Greater Good. Yes, everything sucks, but it's for a reason, and the end justifies the means. Doesn't it?

Things Could Be Worse. Yes, it sucks, but it could be worse. Seen in the contrast between one place and another, or in the contrast between the present and the past.

Fake Utopia. We're fine, everything's perfect. Isn't it? A utopia hiding a darker truth.

Ignorance is Bliss. People are happy due to some kind of mass drugging of the population. Drugs in the drinking water, or subliminal messaging, or similar.

Skeletons in the Closet. The government has a big secret it is desperate to keep under wraps.

Oppressive Government. They have the power, and they certainly like to use it, and abuse it.

Police State. The world is run by a militarised, over-bearing police force.

Criminal Paradise. A place run by criminals, for criminals.

Gang Warfare: The world is run by gangs. They are the law, the order, the judge, and the jury.

We Are Not Alone. A dystopia caused by alien invasion.

Eyes Everywhere. Surveillance is everywhere, constant, and intrusive. The government sees everything.

Out of Bounds. There is a place where no one is ever allowed to go. On pain on death. What's there? I think your main character might be about to find out...

Commercialism Gone Mad. Everyone is constantly bombarded with advertisements. Buy! Buy! Buy!

Capitalism Sucks. A dystopia caused by the characteristics of capitalism.

Life Isn't Fair. A particular group of society is oppressed and discriminated against. This group can be characterised by any common trait.

The Peasants are Revolting. An uprising of the oppressed people.

Polluted Wasteland. You can't breathe the air, or eat the plants, and the animals aren't looking too healthy either.

Industrialisation. The factories don't stop, and neither do the people. It's a life of daily drudgery in the ghetto of industry.

Disposable World. A wasteful world, where everything is throw-away and valueless. Including the people.

Scavenger's Paradise. One man's junk is another man's gold.

Rags and Bones. All that's left is rusty, old rubbish.

Evil Tech. The future is controlled by robots, and they're not very nice.

Nature Fights Back. She's got bored of mankind, so Mother Nature is on the warpath.

Use this space to note down any ideas that have come to you, and to list any of the tropes that you would like to explore.

POPULAR POST-APOCALYPTIC TROPES

The word 'apocalypse', etymologically, means 'revelation', coming from a Greek word meaning 'uncover, reveal'. Despite its ancient origins, the meaning of a catastrophic, earth-ending event didn't develop until the 20th century.

Just like with the dystopian genre, the trends of post-apocalyptica change over time, depending on what is happening in the real world. These trends cluster together, with a particular apocalyptic theme explored over and over, until it's replaced with something else. You can read more about this in the chapters Following Fear Trends and Is the Zombie Genre Dead?

And, as before, many of these tropes can also be found in dystopian fiction.

Take a read through, and see if any of them spark off an idea, whether for now, or for a future story. They can be merged together, or deconstructed, or turned inside-out altogether.

Before...

Panic! Chaos! Everyone knows the end is coming, and the world falls into absolute anarchy.

Rise of the Heroes. The looming end of the world brings out the best in people.

Non Disclosure Agreement. One or more governments are aware that the apocalypse is approaching, and they're trying to stop it, but no one can know about it.

Emergency Broadcast. The government puts out a public broadcast informing the population of the approaching threat.

Let's Get Outta Here. People manage to escape the planet just before it's destroyed.

I'm Not Sick. A lethal pandemic disease threatens humanity. One or more characters are inexplicably immune.

After...

This Place Looks Familiar. It turns out that the desolate, destroyed planet in the story is Earth, after all.

Eternal Winter. Who's up for another ice-age? The last one was fun, right?

Rise of the Animals. Humans are gone, and the animals rise up in their place.

No One Can Hear You Scream. Earth has been destroyed, so what about the astronauts deserted in space?

It's Quiet Here. The world wasn't entirely destroyed, but there aren't many people left on it.

I Think I'm Alone, Now. Someone believes themselves to be the last human on the planet, but then they happen to bump into some more.

Rise and Shine. Somehow, somebody managed to miss the entire apocalypse happening, and wakes up to the aftermath.

A Whole New World. The land was utterly annihilated but, after a few years, it's revived itself, and the inhabitants are returning.

Nuclear Mutants. Radiation creates some nasty monsters.

The Road to Hell. A road jammed full of vehicles abandoned during a mass evacuation. Or, perhaps the drivers are still inside...

Insect Appetisers. Food has become so scarce that people start eating rodents and insects.

Causes...

Crazy Cult. A cult strives to cause the apocalypse.

Reality Tear. Something has gone wrong with the actual fabric of reality itself, and it means certain death and destruction.

Vengeful Gods. A God, a Goddess, a deity, or a group of them bring about the apocalypse.

Device of Destruction. Some kind of device or object is created or discovered that is capable of ending the world.

Big Bang. An explosion so powerful that it destroys the entire planet.

We're Gonna' Need a Bigger Boat. Mass destruction caused by a giant tsunami.

Go To Hell. Hell itself, somehow, manages to invade the world.

Take Us to Your Leader. The world is re-modelled by an invading alien race seeking to take the planet for themselves. The changes don't turn out too well for humans.

Solar Flare. A solar flare hits the planet. It's not good.

The Last Generation. A disease is rendering people sterile. No children, no future.

We Made That. A man-made plague sweeps across the globe. Either released intentionally, or not.

We Don't Talk About It. The cause of the apocalypse is never specified.

The Zombies are Coming. The classic zombie apocalypse.

Again, use this space to note down any ideas that have come to you, and to list any of the tropes that you would like to explore.

THE GENRE PROBLEM

Genre is a classification system for books. Basically, it's to let bookshops know where to shelve your book; be that in an actual, physical shop, or an online shop.

It's also a guide to readers, so that they can quickly find the genre they enjoy.

For authors, agents, and publishers, it helps them to formulate the marketing of the book. It gives them a target demographic of readers to sell to. And that marketing includes things like the blurb, the cover, and even the title itself.

If you plan to pursue a traditional publishing route, via a literary agent and a big publisher, then being true to a single genre can be a huge benefit in the marketability of your book. And that's what the traditional publishing route is looking for.

If you are interested in working with a small, independent press, you have a bit more flexibility on genre. Many independent presses are more willing to take a chance on an unusual book, or a genre-busting book. They tend to accept books they feel passionate about, rather than thinking only of the bottom line.

If you are looking at self-publishing, there are no gatekeepers to tell you to stick to one genre. You are free to write whatever you wish, and ignore any advice that tells you to write to market. You can also place your books into several different genre categories across the various online booksellers.

None of these routes are better than the other. None of these are right, and none are wrong. None are more noble, more professional, or even more lucrative. They are merely different routes. How that path turns out for you is entirely in *how* you choose to walk it, not simply which path you choose.

I write genre mash-ups. I can't help it. It's what makes my heart burn brightest. I could choose to reign myself in, and write to market. To stick, religiously, to the tropes and elements of a single genre. But, I don't. That's my choice, and I live with any consequences of it.

For instance, my dystopian fiction, while set in a future version of earth, always contains magic and paranormal elements. There is futuristic technology, but my books sit far more comfortably within the fantasy genre than the science fiction one. My urban fantasy is always set in a secondary world. That, for some readers, is enough to expel it from the genre altogether. It could possibly be classed as 'cyberpunk', but the heavy magical influence, again, pulls it back towards fantasy. And my post-apocalyptica contains God-like monsters, and is far from your 'typical' rendition of the genre.

You don't need to spend much time around readers, real fanatical readers, to know how strict some of them can be on what they read. If an author dares to break a genre-specific rule, then woe betide them. Many readers will pick up a genre book with a very, very strict set of expectations. And they want those expectations to be met. That's fair enough; it's their reading experience. On the other hand, there are many readers who like to be surprised. Who love to find something totally new and unique within the pages. That's fine too. Again, neither opinion is wrong, neither is better than the other. You just need to decide which readers you are going to aim for.

Let me say this; choosing to write to market is not 'selling out'. It is not an insult or a slap in the face of creative expression. As with the different publishing routes, the choice to write to market is neither more or less noble than writing whatever you want to.

The general opinion in the writing and publishing community is that genre mash-ups tend to be harder to market. As a mixed-bag writer myself, I can attest to the fact that, yes, it can be incredibly difficult. However, the marketing of a single genre book can also be incredibly difficult. The success of a book depends on so, so much more than its content. In fact, the content is probably much further down the list than you would imagine.

Another thing to remember is that the lines between the different genres are not iron rods. They're often more like play-dough. Also, new sub-genres are cropping up all of the time, or breaking away from their parent genres. I've seen many independent authors claim to have penned an entirely new genre altogether.

There will always be readers who are looking for a true recreation of their favourite genre tropes. And there will always be readers looking for something fresh and new. The task of the marketing strategy is always the same: to find the right readers.

To sum up, yes, genre mash-ups are often harder to market, and it is often more difficult to find the right readers for your book. But, they are out there. There might simply be less of them. My advice? Read. Read like crazy. Read all around your genre and keep a list of books that are similar to yours. Also, ask your readers which authors they think your books are similar to. Base your marketing strategy on this.

Also, if you're doing something totally new with genre, don't be afraid to do something totally new with your marketing. However cringe-worthy the phrase is; think outside of the box. Look for opportunities beyond the norm, and make your own opportunities. One thing I have learnt through my publishing career is just to ask. If you want something, just ask for it. The worst anyone can say is "No".

Use the following space for any thoughts you have on genre. Write down the elements of your favourite genres, and think about whether you will look to stick to them, or create a whole new flavour.

FOLLOWING FEAR TRENDS

I've already mentioned that the subject matter of genres such as dystopia and post-apocalypse tend to follow particular trends. Those trends can be tracked through our culture's history, and the events that were occurring at those times.

Taking in books, movies, and television, we've seen groupings of subject matters such as robot uprisings, nuclear war, alien invasions, and pandemic diseases.

Any creative person is the product of the many influences pressing upon them, and their art is a reflection of those influences. One of those influences is events happening in the world around them, while another is the popular culture that they consume.

There are trend-chasers: when they see that a particular piece of media is popular, they seek to meet the desires of that same audience. To piggy-back on the success of the original media. We've seen this happen over and over, throughout history, and across the entire spectrum of creative mediums. After all, humans learn through imitation. Babies learn to smile, to walk, to speak because they are copying what everyone around them is doing. As adults, we continue to learn in the same way. And chasing a large, ready-made audience makes very good business sense.

But what made that first piece of media so popular? Of course, a large part of it is marketing. A large marketing budget, and a clever marketing campaign can make a huge difference. But, still, that piece of media, and its marketing campaign is, somehow, hitting the exact right notes at the exact right time. It is speaking to people in a language they understand. It is mirroring something already inside of them.

We've seen small-budget movies do this, suddenly rising to popularity the creators probably never dreamed of. And we've seen huge budget movies fall flat because they didn't carry the right message. Or, they came at the wrong time.

I'm sure that you can think of a book, or movie, or TV show that seemed to appear from nowhere and rise to the top of the pile, even if it didn't appear to deserve the spot. And, honestly, a lot of it is pure luck.

The real key, of course, is predicting what the next trend will be, rather than trying to grab the coat-tails of the ones that are already running. You cannot predict the future. But you can certainly try. And predicting the future starts with the present. What are people afraid of right now? What possible threats are just emerging? What leaps are being made in medicine, science, space travel, that could have scary consequences?

The other important place to start is with you. However much us writers may like to hide away in our own offices and writing nooks, we are still members of society, however inactively. What worries do you have for the future? What dangerous paths can you see humankind stepping onto?

Of course, any of these fear trends may be short-lived, giving your book an unspoken sell-by-date. There are other subjects that recur over and over, and others that tend to be somewhat evergreen and constant.

Having said all of this, the one thing to always remember is that, no matter the focus of the fear, or the threat in your book, you are writing about PEOPLE. You are writing about people facing a danger, and those people, somehow, overcoming it. No matter the cause, that is a subject that will, forever and always, speak to your readers.

Whether you choose to look for a particular 'hot topic', or wish to speculate what will be popular next year, you need to be focussing on your characters. Focussing on their emotions, their relationships, their strengths and weaknesses, and the way in which they overcome their flaws.

Write some notes in the space below about the kind of threats you are interested in writing about. Make some notes about what scares you.

MAKING MONSTERS

Something I absolutely love doing is dreaming up my own monsters. I'm a total worldbuilding nerd, and my favourite part of worldbuilding is creating belief systems. Be that religion and spirituality, or myths and legends. And monsters belong in all of those places.

Every culture in the world has its traditional monsters, branching throughout all of history. There are monsters that live in our world, and monsters that visit from other realms and dimensions. There are monsters that walk among humans, unnoticed and unseen, while there are others that isolate themselves away from humankind. There are monsters that can be captured or vanquished, and those that can never, and will never, be stopped.

Many monsters act as a warning, or a threat for bad behaviour, especially those in stories told to children. They are used to represent sinful actions or traits, and they are used to keep people away from danger. Whether that danger be physical risk, or a more metaphorical danger with the threat of eternal damnation.

Other monsters are simply there to remind us that we are not the most powerful beings in existence. That we, too, are mortal, and further down the food chain than we like to accept.

These are the monsters of myth and legend. The monsters that, as we grow older, are easier to shrug off as just being shadows, or the wind howling outside. They are the monsters of conspiracy theories, able to be ignored through the ridicule of those who still believe in them. There is great comfort in being able to laugh at a monster, and to write it off as nothing more than a childish fairytale.

But, as we all know, there are some monsters who are very, very real. And they are the most terrifying of all. Because those monsters look exactly like us. Because they are us.

There is little more monstrous than what man has done to its fellow man. There are countless examples of monstrous behaviour, whether individual, or institutional, throughout the history of every country. And those examples aren't confined to history, either. They still happen, every day, all around us.

And these monstrous acts, carried out by humans who, on the outside, look no more extraordinary than you or I, also serve as a reminder. A reminder that all of us have the potential to be monsters.

If you're having non-human monsters in your story, you may choose to use recognisable ones such as vampires and werewolves. There are always new things to do with such creatures, and fresh angles to explore.

You may wish to borrow from myth, possibly using an obscure, unknown cryptid, or mixing different ones together. You'll find creatures across the world with similar traits, themes, and motives, even if they look completely different.

You may prefer to create a monster of your own, entirely from scratch. In which case, existing legends are a great place to start. Look at what exists, how it exists, where it loiters, and build from there. If you let yourself be inspired by existing myth, then your finished monster will feel authentic and ancient, while also being something new and original.

Look at how the monsters tie into your story. Which of your characters are at threat from them? What themes and metaphors does the creature represent, and how does this fit in with your story? You want to match and integrate your monster so that another couldn't take its place.

Think about their role in your society. Are they legends, or fairytales, only believed in by children? Or are they real, and present, and visible? Perhaps monsters are trying to integrate into society, or maybe they're treated like unwelcome outsiders. Maybe they're hunted, or captured, or domesticated. Maybe they're experimented on, or gazed at in zoos, or treated with great reverence and respect.

Every side character in your story should be just as fleshed out, just as authentic and real, as the main character. Side characters are, in their own minds, the heroes of their own stories. This is no different when you're creating monsters, whether human or not.

These creatures have backstories, and histories that have led them to this point. That have led them to the monstrous act they are about to perform. They have motivations, influences, and goals, whether they be base, survival instincts, or more complex reasoning.

A person can do an evil, cruel thing and truly, honestly believe that they are, in fact, doing a good thing. Or doing a bad thing for the right reasons. Or that it is for the greater good. They may feel that they have been backed into a corner, and that they're choosing the lesser of two evils. Or that they have been left with no option but to fight their way out, fighting for their own survival regardless of their victims.

Sometimes, people make awful mistakes. Sometimes, they are acting on remembered responses, protecting themselves from hurt that they have felt before. Sometimes, it's just as self-destructive as it is harmful to others.

When you've worked hard to create a main cast, a story, and a world that is fully rounded, and believable, and immersive, you don't want to bolt on a thin, shallow monster for no other reason than shock value. Ensure that you're making that monster believable, that it represents the themes of your book, and that it really feels like it belongs there.

Because that is what truly makes monsters scary; the fear that you can't remove them.

Because they belong there, just as much as you do.

Use the space below to make some notes about monsters. Any ideas you've had while reading this, or anything you'd like to research or to develop further.

IS THE ZOMBIE GENRE DEAD?

I am a big fan of the zombie genre, and it's been with us for a very, very long time.

Zombie-type folklore has existed in parts of the world for several centuries, and the first novels exploring the idea were published back in the 1920s, with the first movies arriving just a decade later.

It's a theme that keeps being repeated, often in those trend clusters I've already spoken about, particularly when you're looking at the cause of the zombie outbreak.

It is often said, by various noteworthy people, that the zombie genre has reached its limits. That everything that can be done with it, has been done with it. That it has lost its relevance. But, whenever this viewpoint is rolled out again, someone releases a book, or a movie, or a TV show, to prove otherwise.

In fact, the zombie genre never loses its relevance, and is particularly important in today's world.

Whether alien interference, magical intervention, or a new vaccine gone horribly wrong, zombies keep, quite literally, rising from the dead to haunt us over and over. It may be a virus outbreak, whether man-made or not, whether intentional or not. It may be a toxic gas illegally used in a war. It may be an experiment with unintended consequences.

In a world where science and medicine advances so quickly, and far outstrips the general population's understanding, the zombie genre can thrive. In a world where we're creating vaccines, and the population is so viciously divided on their benefits, the zombie genre is so relevant. We're travelling further into space, deeper underground, and the melting of polar ice is uncovering things completely alien to our world. We're making life, and taking life away, and heading towards a point of no return with climate change. All of this is fantastic fodder for a zombie apocalypse.

Fear exists in bubbles of misunderstanding and misconception. Humans fear the other, and fear the unknown. And we often despise in others the qualities we refuse to accept in ourselves. These are the places in which monsters exist. In the shadows within us. In the secrets we keep, and in the parts of us that we bury. In our shame, in our regrets, in our fear of what we might become.

Zombies are so recognisable to us. Quite literally, in many cases, they are members of our own family, friends, neighbours. Zombies blur the line between friend and foe. They exist as both simultaneously. Just as they are, simultaneously, human and non-human.

Zombies are so feared, and such a popular, recurring creature, because they are so confronting to us. Because they represent two huge things that we are, but that we refuse to accept about ourselves.

Zombies, first of all, are the embodiment of our own mortality. For most of us, death is kept at arm's length. It's veiled, it's locked into a box, and it's buried deep underground. We concentrate on remembering our lost loved ones as they were in life, rather than think about them in death. We imagine an afterlife where we will be reunited with them. Zombies force us to confront our own mortality. Our own deaths are, literally, walking towards us, seeking to devour us. That is something we would rather not have to face. In any capacity.

Second, zombies represent the fact that we are animals. That we are subject and slave to our base instincts. Instincts of survival, instincts to feed, to reproduce, and to do so single-mindedly. Zombies are humans with their humanity removed. Devolved and reduced to base animal instincts. This state is something we like to think that we have evolved so far beyond, that we wouldn't ever return to it.

But, we see this base behaviour around us everyday. Mindless greed exercised without empathy. We deplore it, and condemn it, in an effort to distance ourselves from it. So that we can say "But I'm not like that. I'd never be like that." And, when we're talking about such behaviour, we're not referring merely to rogue individuals. It's not just rare, criminal 'sociopaths'. This behaviour is often institutional, and carried out on a large scale. By corporations, by governments, by entire societies.

This is why zombies will never lose their relevance. And, as society evolves, as we move forward and our world changes, so will our zombies. Their source will change, their image will change, and the solution will change. The metaphor, however, will always be the same.

CREATING HISTORIES

When you're creating a dystopian vision of the future, society is very unlikely to have changed from what it is today, to what your vision is, overnight. There would have been a series of steps to create the change. The change may have been rapid, coming about in just a few years, or it may have taken several generations, or even centuries to become what it has become.

There may have been a catalyst moment, a catastrophe, a worldwide event, that caused it, but no entire society, along with its infrastructure, can be remodelled in a day. Likewise, it can't rebuild and settle into a new norm instantly. Such changes take time, leadership, co-operation, and enforcement.

If you're writing a post-apocalyptic world, things may be a little different, depending on the type of apocalypse, the timeline of your story, and the amount of warning people were given.

You may choose an apocalyptic event which is instant, with the effects hitting straight away. Natural disasters, alien invasion, worldwide nuclear war. This may have been foreseen (whether by conspiracy theorists, doom-dayers, or survivalists brushed off as crazy, or by scientists working alongside the governments), or it may have come as a complete and total surprise to everyone.

Alternatively, you may choose more of a slow-burning apocalypse. Perhaps a worldwide pandemic that evolves into a zombie apocalypse, or a catastrophic climate change event. It's important to remember, that the soul of the apocalyptic genre exists in a place of shock, and panic, and rapid change. If your apocalypse is too slow-burning, you're moving away from what the genre is all about. Your readers want to see a quick collapse of the world we know, and they want to see characters fighting to adapt to, and exist in, a totally new world.

When you're devising your apocalyptic or dystopian timeline, you need to decide where along it your story will sit. Will you write about the build up to the change, and show your characters fighting against it, trying to stop it, or helplessly watching society begin to crumble? Or will you set your story in the middle of it all? Will you show your characters fighting zombies, or leading violent rebellions? Alternatively, you may choose to focus on the aftermath, whether immediate, or many years down the line.

You may even want to jump around in time, using flashbacks, or other non-linear story concepts. If you decide to do this, make sure that you know what you're doing. That you've looked at how other authors have made this work, and that you know *why* you want to do it. If you know the effect you want to create, then you can work out how best to do it.

Your timeline is so important in these genres, because the contrast between then and now is absolutely vital to highlighting the dystopian or post-apocalyptic nature of the world your characters are living in. Your readers need to see that the world has changed, and how much it has changed, and, most of all, how your characters are dealing with that change.

When you're looking at the timeline of your world, remember to think about all the different things that affect it, as well as all the different things that it affects. When you change one thing in a society, you change so many other things too. Remember what I said earlier about imagining your world as a pool. When you drop in a pebble, you cause ripples. Sometimes, those ripples fade out quickly, others keep going for years. Some ripples can even become tsunamis.

Let's look at an example of these ripples. If, for instance, you remove women from the workplace, how does that affect the economy? Who replaces them? Do you need a huge influx of immigrants to take up their posts? How are families affected when they suddenly have to cope with a single income, or no income at all? How does it affect welfare, or the housing market? What happens to the education of girls? If they're removed from the education system, what happens to all the redundant teachers, both male and female? How does society cope with the sudden loss of expertise? What happens with women in prisons, and how does it affect crime? How is the retraining of men to replace women handled? Who pays for it? Then you have the whole issue of gender. Who decides who is, and isn't, a woman?

The ripples go out, and out, and out. If you're writing about a singular country, how does it fit in with the rest of the world? How is trade affected, and international relations, and defence? Is this country sanctioned for its policy changes, or does it lead the way in worldwide change?

Likewise, with an apocalyptic event, everything you change, changes everything else. If you remove huge numbers of the human population, what happens to each country's infrastructure? What happens to the electricity supply, the food supply, economics? How does nature respond? What happens to the dead, and how is the spread of disease handled?

If you remove half of the landmass with sea level rises, how is land ownership dealt with? What happens to people already living in a different country to their birthplace or place of citizenship? How do the remaining countries exist alongside each other? Do countries band together, or shut themselves off to protect their precious resources? What happens with the countries that have disappeared entirely?

There is so much to think about when you're constructing your world's timeline, although, you don't need to panic over all of the tiny details. It's good to think about these things, but, unless it matters to the story, it's not always vital that you have all of the answers. What is more important, is that you write amazing characters on compelling journeys.

I want you to think about these things to get your ideas flowing, and to think about the impact any small change can, potentially, have. Don't get overwhelmed, and don't fall into the trap of doing so much in-depth worldbuilding, that you never get around to actually writing the story. Above everything else, get your story written.

There are plenty of very successful dystopian and post-apocalyptic stories that offer up no backstory, or no explanation at all. An unknown apocalyptic event, or a dystopian future that just is. It is absolutely fine to leave your readers pondering over such matters, as long as you give them a believable immersive world, an engrossing story, and sympathetic, relatable characters that they want to see succeed.

Just be aware that, like everything else in your writing, ambiguity is a delicate balance. Too much, and your readers will feel confused and unfulfilled. But when you tip the scale too far the other way, you're at risk of boring your readers with info dumps and complex history lessons.

Getting the balance right isn't something that you can expect to simply get spot-on first time. Like all aspects of writing, it's something that develops as your writing skills mature. Read, practice, and go with your gut. Beta and early readers will let you know if you've got the balance off. Don't stress over it too much, and certainly not during the first draft. I'll say it again; just get your story written.

MAPPING YOUR FUTURE

If I scared you a little in the last chapter, I hope you can forgive me in this one. I have an exercise for you which is about freeing your mind, and going absolutely crazy over potential story lines. Just going mad with it, and letting yourself loose without any holding back at all.

When you're creating a dystopian or post-apocalyptic world, as I've already said, the important thing is to show a stark, fundamental difference between the way the world was before, and the way it is after. Therefore, no matter when along the timeline you choose to set your story, you want to start with today. With the way the world is right now. Every possible future, every potential reality, starts now. In this very moment.

You can complete this exercise whether you already have an idea of what you want to write about, or if you haven't made any decisions, or had any ideas yet.

I tend to do this as a spider diagram, starting in the centre, and working my way out in a web from there. It gives me an opportunity to explore various different threads. Different possible outcomes and timelines. That way, it could throw up a potential future that I hadn't previously thought of, and surprise me with a whole new timeline. But, if you prefer a different layout, that's fine, go with whatever makes you happy.

If you really let your imagination go wild, really wild, you never know what might pop out. Sure, a lot of it might be unsuitable, or not what you want to write about, or downright stupid, but who cares? No one will ever see this diagram except for you. And, if you think you've taken things to far, you can always reign it back in.

Start in the centre of the page. That way, you can extend out in any direction, giving you an entire spread of possibilities. Somewhere in the centre, write down a problem in the world today. Or a potential problem. Something happening that could be leading mankind down a very slippery slope. Think of something that interests you, or angers you, or puts a fire in your belly. Be it an issue of inequality, or health, or technology, or the climate, or economics.

Take that issue and push the possible outcome to the extreme. Create stepping stones leading from the initial issue, out, and out, and out, to the most extreme future that you can imagine.

Maybe genetics research leads to half human, half animal hybrids. Perhaps the cost of education leads to computer chips inserted into people's brains. Maybe space exploration causes the death of the sun. Go mad, go crazy, and take it to the extreme. You can always pull it back.

When you've finished exploring the raw ideas, you can decide which story thread you'd like to explore further. You can also decide whereabouts along that timeline you want to place your story. Go for it. Don't limit yourself. Have fun.

BACKWARDS ENGINEERING YOUR WORLD

So far, I've spoken a lot about the source, and the starting point of your world. About tracking the future forwards, from today. I work in a very linear fashion. I write my books in order, from beginning to end, but not everyone works like that. That being said, I often come up with ideas, and I have to backwards engineer them. Let me explain...

Sometimes, you might come up with the idea for your future world first. Your 'what if'. Rather than working forwards, from the start of the problem, and exploring where it might end up, you may need to do things backwards. This is absolutely fine, and no less successful than doing things forwards.

If you come up with your vision of the future, and then want to fill in the history, it's not too far different than doing it forwards. Make the future your starting point; the world you want to create. And then ask yourself "Why? Why is the world like this? What happened to cause it?" Work your way backwards with the same stepping stones.

Instead of asking "What happens if I change this?" you need to ask yourself "What changed to cause this?" We're still playing with the same pebbles making the same ripples, you're simply fishing them back out of the water, instead of dropping them in.

This is also a really handy way to deal with 'cool things' that you think of, and simply have to include in your story. It might be a piece of futuristic tech, or an odd little nuance of your society, or a common phrase that people use. It might be the name of a place, or a seemingly irrelevant, yet dominant organisation.

It is absolutely fine to include things in your world, simply because the idea excites you. Even if, when you decide on it, you're not entirely sure how it fits into your worldbuilding. Because it's these little details, these unique things, these punch-the-air moments, and ideas that will simply make your readers smile, it's these things that really fill out your world, and put your stamp on it. They make your world a place readers want to dive into, want to live in, and want to read more about.

By backwards engineering these things, you can truly integrate them into your world, and make it look like they always belonged there. They won't stand out, you're not marking them with red flags and an obvious statement of "Hey, look at this cool thing I put in, aren't I awesomely clever?" Because that's not awesomely clever. Red flagging things in your book will pull your audience out of the illusion. It will jolt them back to reality and remind them that they are simply reading a book, written, apparently, by a writer who cared more about looking smart, or witty, than they cared about keeping the reader immersed in the story.

When you're backwards engineering, and working out a plausible reason for the things you want to include, and giving them a realistic, believable history, you want to integrate them as fully into the history of your world as you can. Make it seem that society couldn't have possibly evolved the way it did, without this particular thing.

This is especially important if this thing you want to include is the way in which your main character finally vanquishes their foes, and achieves their goal. A conveniently placed object, person, or situation, that suddenly materializes in order to save the day, is known as 'deus ex machina', or 'god from the machine'. Unless being used for comedic effect, it will cause your readers to roll their eyes, toss your book away, and claim the ending 'ruined'.

That's why it's important to integrate everything into the history of your world. If there is a weapon, a magical ability, a skill, an ally, whatever it is, if the main character needs something like this to achieve their goal, it has to be foreshadowed. It has to crop up in the story beforehand. It needs to be weaved, seamlessly, into the fabric of the world, the story, and your character.

You can have surprises, and turn-arounds, and you can wrench the rug out from under the feet of your readers, but it needs to be something they can trace back. You want them to say "Aha! So *that's* why that was there!" You don't want them saying "What? Are you serious? That would never happen!"

You'd be amazed at the seemingly outlandish things you can get away with, as long as they are integrated into the story properly. A reader will happily suspend their disbelief to accept dragons or unicorns or huge sea monsters. They won't do it if your character turns out to be amazing at martial arts that they have never been trained in.

NATURAL AND MAN-MADE DISASTERS

Both natural disasters, and man-made ones, are regular features in post-apocalyptic stories, but they also crop up in dystopias too. Sometimes, a natural disaster is set off by man's interference, even when they're trying to do some good.

As a species, we're something of a plague on this planet. If the history of the earth, its entire lifetime, were condensed into just 24 hours, humans have existed for less than 2 minutes. Yet, in that time, we've claimed the planet for ourselves, claimed dominion over every inch of it, and every other living thing, and changed it forever. We have caused the extinction of hundreds of vertebrate species. And we're not finished yet.

We've dug out the minerals, we've flattened hills and mountains, we've re-routed rivers, and we've destroyed forests. We've replaced grass with concrete, we've drained marshlands and pooled water into reservoirs. We've even littered outer space with debris and rubbish. We've torn holes in the ozone, and set about fixing them again.

But, at the same time, we've explored, and discovered, and learnt so much about the planet on which we reside. And beyond. It still amazes me that we know how much the earth weighs. Near enough, at least. We've learnt about plants and animals, and we've learnt to love them, and revere them, and care for them.

We may be slow to act, and it often feels like a losing battle, but there are people, and a growing amount of them, who want to reverse the bad effects. Unfortunately, our good intentions can be the very thing that sets off the disaster, and there are several stories that explore just that idea.

Humans like to imagine that they sit at the top of the food chain. We don't. We may have increased our chances with weapons, but there are plenty of things on this planet that are bigger, stronger, and hungrier than we are. And the majority of people aren't walking around with loaded guns.

This is why the monster stories prevail. The story of the big, bad wolf. Or crocodile. Or shark. Or whatever. These stories have been with us since humans first picked up charcoal and drew on the walls of their caves. It's less of an immediate danger to most of us, these days, than it used to be, but it's still there. We still hear of hikers attacked by mountain lions, and campers killed by bears. You can then add in the fact that many cities have zoos, and there are regular occurrences of animals escaping.

There are stories of big cats roaming wild in the UK. Escaped, or set loose, from private collections of exotic animals, kept before the introduction of the Dangerous and Wild Animals Act in 1976. Having grown up on the edge of Dartmoor, Devon, these are stories that are of particular interest to me. I grew up with tales of the 'Dartmoor Beast', and often scoured the moors in hope of seeing a glimpse of it.

But it's not just creatures with big teeth and claws that might want to hunt us down.

Put small creatures, even insects, in a large enough group, and you can unleash a destructive, even deadly, plague. The devastation caused to crops—a whole population's food supply—by locusts is very real, and very deadly. You also get the added bonus of the creep-out factor, and of hitting people's phobias right in the gut. Spiders, cockroaches, moths and butterflies. Maggots, worms, and lice. I'm getting all itchy just thinking about it!

Beyond creatures, whether cute and cuddly or creepy-crawly, nature itself can seek its revenge.

We have a very mistaken idea that we are greater than Mother Nature herself. That we can control her, and bend her to our will. But the lady hits back, and she hits back hard. No matter what humans do, however many rivers we re-route, however strong or flexible our buildings are, we are still utterly at her mercy. Floods, fires, hurricanes, earthquakes, volcanoes, landslides. She has an entire arsenal. All she needs to do is blow hard enough, and she can blow us away. She can ruin crops, spread disease, poison, and destroy us.

Add in the interference of mankind: building on flood plains, hollowing out mountains, and the ever-disastrous introducing of non-native species, and we are really pushing our luck. We're practically goading nature to fight back.

There are many books, movies, and TV shows that see nature striking back in new ways. Adapting to kill us, whether paranormally or through accelerated evolution. To become deadly. Be it a new disease, plants turning sapient, or killer rain. Create an air-born attack on us, and there's not a huge amount that we can do. This is why so many post-apocalyptic and dystopian futures see humans cowering underground, unable to exist on the surface anymore.

Of course, it might not be our fault at all. A solar flare, an asteroid strike, a geomagnetic reversal of the poles. There have been several ice ages through the planet's history. They happened before we were here, so it wouldn't, necessarily, be our fault if it happened again. Many people argue that the current warming of our planet is unrelated to our existence. You could also have some kind of alien or deity interference.

It all depends on what you want to say. What message you want to put across. Do you want to warn mankind that they are causing their own destruction? Do you want to show that we're just tiny, insignificant creatures at the mercy of nature? Do you want to explore the notion that everything is completely random and we have no control over anything? Do you want to say that there is something far, far bigger than us at play?

Of course, you may just have a cool idea that you want to have fun with. That's fine too. But a message will still come through to your readers, whether you set out with one in mind, or not.

It's handy to be aware of the message you're putting across with your book, even if it's a consideration only with hindsight, after having written the first draft. Some writers like to plan out their books' themes and ideas, while others prefer to simply write, and see what comes up.

It may not even be until you hand your book over to beta readers that you realise the true themes and messages of your book. After all, readers often find themes and associations that the writer never intended and was unaware of. Because we all approach books from our own, unique, point of view. Books speak to us all in different ways. As Edmund Wilson stated; "No two persons ever read the same book."

METAPHOR AND SOCIAL COMMENTARY

I talked a little in the previous chapter about your book's themes, and the message it portrays to readers. Post-apocalyptic and dystopian books often stand as a strong message to humanity. They are depicting an undesirable, unfair, even deadly future for mankind, and, by their very nature, become something of a warning.

Because the unpleasant world they portray is in the future, whether near-future or centuries down the line, there is still a chance for people to avoid ending up in such a place.

While authors may simply want to write a fun, exciting story that caught their imagination, without any kind of agenda or comment on society as it is today, it is a genre which is often interpreted with a deeper meaning. Whether intended, or not.

If you think back to the spider diagram you drew earlier, the stepping stones between the world today, and the unpleasant future you imagine, what you are essentially doing is exaggerating a problem, or potential problem, that you see around you. You're highlighting it, inviting deeper scrutiny of it, red-flagging it for investigation.

As I state on my own website; 'Through my fiction, I seek to highlight the social and cultural rules that we accept without question. Sometimes, without even noticing. Fiction offers a unique platform to do this, with dystopia at the fore. By exaggerating these ingrained rules, or by reversing them entirely, we can start to examine them. And question them. And challenge those that are harmful.'

I always tell people that, if they want to know my political stance, they only need to read my books.

Dystopian futures tend to hinge on inequality and unfairness. They tend to pitch one demographic against another: rich against poor, rebels against the establishment. It doesn't take much deviation from the perceived norm to be considered a rebel. Think about the society and culture you currently live in. It may seem liberal, and, to a certain extent, free, but when you really start to look at it, you might find some aspects that surprise you.

Look at how 'the other' is treated. People of colour, people with a different religion, cultural background, or first language. Think about groups of people with different political allegiances, and how those groups interact with one another. Even the different generations. You need look no further than social media to find division. The comments and posts you'll find may display a scary amount of hatred, with insults, and even physical threats, thrown back and forth. Arguing about gender identity, sexuality, or even the latest company to release a vegan food alternative.

It really doesn't take much to be considered a rebel from the norm. An alternative. The other. An outsider.

Throughout history, terrifying things have happened to those rebels in society. Let's quickly look at women. Around about half the population of the world is female. Despite this, the majority of the world's land and wealth is owned by men. Women are more likely to be unemployed, or employed in low-paid, vulnerable work. Women are often perceived as being the minority. As being 'the other'.

Throughout history, women have been expected to adhere to a tight definition of behaviour. A definition set by patriarchal societies. Those who lived outside the norm, whether by choice, or not, were burnt as witches, or thrown into asylums. It has been very, very easy for a woman to become a rebel, and the consequences are often disproportionate to the crime.

Think of the world as it is today. Women can 'rebel' in the slightest of ways. By choosing not to have children. By choosing reusable nappies, by breastfeeding in public, by choosing to go back to work, or by choosing to be a stay-at-home parent. They can rebel by demanding equal pay, even if it's shrouded in their country's law. By seeking education, by driving, by speaking out. We can see examples of this across the entire world, in every culture, even in those that we would consider 'liberal' and 'fair'.

And, it's good to remember, that the biggest, most rebellious, most dangerous thing any member of 'the other' can ever do, is to demand change. To demand equality. We've seen this in every equal rights struggle that has happened, in every one that is still happening. And it will continue to happen. The most rebellious thing 'the other' can do is to stand up and claim to be equal. Claim to be human too.

Think about who the other is in your dystopia. The defining feature that makes someone the other can be anything. It might be something they can't change, such as biological factors. Or it might be something that they can change. Or, at least, that the ruling class believes they can change. Why are they seen as the other? What is the punishment for being the other? And what are they going to do about it?

When you're creating a post-apocalyptic society, all of the rules can be different. While dystopias tend to be an exaggeration of the world as we see it today, a future that can be tracked back to now, an apocalyptic event can change everything. It can take society so far away from its current position, and so quickly, that it's barely recognisable.

However, one thing will always be recognisable: people, and the way that they are.

I'll say it again: no matter what story you're writing, no matter what future you're creating, you are, first and foremost, writing about the people in it. The story is always, and must always, be about the characters.

When tragedies happen, when the unprecedented happens, when the terrifying, unimaginable, and unexpected happens, people react in different ways. There are those who will fall apart. Those who see the new future as completely unmanageable, those who cannot see a way to exist in it. Those who choose to bow out of life altogether. There are those who will try their best to carry on as normal. Those who find comfort in routine and ritual. There are those that see the new world as an opportunity. Who refuse to let it beat them, and rise to the challenge. Within that group, there are those who will strive to make things better. The challenge will bring out the best in them. And there are those who will be selfish, and bend the new world to their own benefit, no matter who they hurt along the way.

People will always be people, no matter what they're facing.

Humans tend to be social creatures. Herd animals. They believe that there is 'safety in numbers'. Loners tend to be seen as 'the other'. As the rebels.

As a species, humans tend to cling to people they feel alike to. The camaraderie between the perceived 'same' is evident at any sports event, or music concert. When you walk down the street and spot someone wearing a t-shirt depicting a movie you love, you feel an instant bond. If only for a fleeting moment. I suppose it's because we assume that we know these people, at least in part, that we feel safer with them. The other is an unknown. A wildcard. You can't be sure how they might react, and so, you can't trust them. However wrong, however incorrect and harmful it is, this reaction is part of our defence mechanism. A primitive instinct.

Can we rise above such an instinct? Can we evolve beyond it, or are we bound by it? As an author, that's your decision to make.

FINDING THE HOPE AND THE HEROES

Many people think of dystopian and post-apocalyptic worlds as being devoid of hope. As being dark, depressing places, without light, or happiness, or any prospect of improvement. That is not how I view such worlds.

I view dystopia and post-apocalypse as very hopeful, positive genres. Perhaps I'm just an incurable optimist, but bear with me a moment.

For one thing, you're depicting a future that hasn't happened yet. A future that we may yet be able to avoid. A future that, if we can become better humans, we can certainly avoid. Of course, there's always the chance we might not, and that we're stumbling towards some terrible future with little care to turn back. But we're not there yet. And, until we are, there is always hope.

While, certainly, these genres can stand as a horrible, stark warning for humanity to change its ways, they also stand as an example of how to change. And as inspiration to do so.

There's nothing like taking the most marginalised, persecuted character, facing them with insurmountable barriers, with unbeatable foes, and watching them succeed nonetheless. Because if they can do it, there's hope for us too.

When you write a story, the absolute crux of it, the most important aspect, is the character's journey. The ways in which they change to face their foes, and the ways in which their foes change them. The things they learn about themselves, the hidden traits that rise to the top.

It's commonly said that people really learn who they are, what kind of person they are, when they're faced with their greatest challenges. Put people under pressure, and they either crack and break, or they harden into diamonds. You know; those kind of sayings that are pasted over photos of mountains or sunrises, and shared around on social media. They may induce cynical eye-rolling, but they really are true. No one knows how they will react in a certain situation, especially when that situation is something they have never faced before. Perhaps, even, no one in the history of the world has ever faced it.

Perhaps they will discover that they are a hero, after all.

When tragedies happen in the world, there are people who will run towards the event, as well as those who run away. Running from danger is an instinct. It's a natural response. In most cases, it is the most useful, the most helpful, and the safest option. It lowers the number of casualties, and leaves space for trained professionals to do exactly what they are trained to do.

Yet, the idea of an untrained hero, an 'average Joe', who takes it upon themselves to step in, and step up, has become a wonderfully romanticised idea. In fact, many, many lives have actually been saved by these unexpected heroes.

Of course, heroism takes different forms. There's the kind of heroism when someone tackles a gunman to the ground. There's the kind of heroism when someone saves a field of horses from rising flood waters. There's the kind of heroism when someone regularly checks in on an elderly neighbour.

Heroism doesn't have to be guns blazing. It doesn't have to be loud, and public, and awe-inspiring. It can be quiet, and personal, and tender. Heroism can be a whisper passing through a crowd. It can be one hand taking hold of another. It can be a smile, a nod, a look that simply says 'I believe in you'. Heroism can simply be someone stepping out of their front door.

Taking your no-one-special character, and placing them at the front of a revolutionary uprising, or having them save the entire planet, makes for a truly exciting story. But they can be heroes in other ways, too. Perhaps their heroism is to change. To believe in something better. Perhaps their act of heroism is to help a reader to feel less alone.

You don't need to put a gun in the hand of your hero. It can be just as powerful to have them hold a flower.

CREATING SURVIVORS

I always joke that I wouldn't last five minutes in a post-apocalyptic world. I'm not very practical, I don't have many (or even any) useful skills, I have very little common sense, and I tend to panic. Also, I'm naive, a total empath, and tend to think with my heart instead of my head. It would be very, very easy to lure me into a trap with a child or animal supposedly needing help.

My instinct, in such a situation, would be to seek out sanctuary with others. I would never survive on my own. Likewise, all of your characters will come into the situation with their own level of skills, personality traits, and likelihood of making it through to the end.

For one thing, there's the big difference between people who are forced to adapt to a new world, and those who have been born into it. When your characters are born into a dystopian world, it is their norm, no matter how they feel about it, or how much they strive to change it. They have guidance on how to survive there from their parents.

In contrast, people surviving an apocalyptic event, or living through a societal shift into a harsh dystopia, are forced to adapt. To change the way they live, the way they view the world. They might need to completely adjust their attitude towards strangers, or rewrite their own moral compass. They might have to become a different person entirely.

There are people who appear to be well-placed for surviving an apocalypse. People with wilderness skills, or fighting skills, or a high level of practicality, logic, and common sense. Some people just seem to be very adaptable, able to think on their feet, and improvise. However, this doesn't always make a survivor.

There are many useful traits that a survivor can have. They might be cynical and untrusting of people, and that trait, once considered to be a flaw, can suddenly be the one thing that keeps them alive. They might be meticulous, measured, and painstakingly conscientious. In a previous time, these traits may have alienated them, and annoyed people, but they may become the desired traits for a good leader.

Survivors aren't necessarily the fastest, or the strongest, or even the smartest. Sometimes, the survivor might be the smallest, and the quietest, and the stillest. Someone able to disappear in the shadows, and to slip by unnoticed. They may be the ones that draw the least attention. They may be the ones refusing to abandon their sense of humanity.

Think wide and broad about the idea of a survivor, and think, deeply, about the traits that might help someone to survive in the particular world that you have built. Create characters that will thrive in your world, even if they might have completely faltered in the world as it used to be.

Think about inner strength, as well as outer strength. Think about mental speed, as well as physical speed. Think about emotional abilities as well as wilderness skills.

Consider the unlikely survivors. The ones that get by with cunning, or subtlety, or sheer dumb luck. Consider the surprise survivors, and the ones that survive under the radar.

Remember, of course, to look at your character's arc, their journey. Do they become more capable, more practical, through your book? Do they find that the traits they always saw as weaknesses, are actually their strengths? Do they discover that the skills they learnt, and all of the preparations that they made, are actually useless? Do they discover that they are, in fact, after all, a survivor? And that they actually want to survive?

In dystopian and post-apocalyptic worlds, you can push characters to their very limits, and discover where their limits actually are. You can break them, rebuild them, and break them again. You can discover their true spirits, and you can show them who they really are, even if it comes as a surprise.

CHARACTER ARCS AND WORLD ARCS

Your characters are the reason your readers keep turning the pages. Why they keep coming back to your stories, and buying your books. You can write the most exciting plots in the world, but your readers need to care about the characters to keep reading. They need to fall in love with them, and really want to see them succeed.

You want your readers to feel excited as your characters fight their enemies. You want them to be terrified when your characters are in danger. Fearful that they won't achieve their goal. And you want them to feel triumphant when they do. It is all of those emotions that keep readers invested in your books. And those emotions will only come when they care.

You want to carry your readers along through the whole book, or series, and to do that, you need an arc for them to travel along. You need a story arc, leading them from the beginning to the end, and you need a character arc. A journey that your character takes. One that your readers can join them on.

This may simply be a metaphorical journey, or it may be an actual, physical one, with them travelling great distances across your world. Even if they are embarking on a literal journey, they need to take a metaphorical one too. One of self discovery. One that changes them forever. One on which they can grow as a person, and become something they weren't before. Or become more of what they were.

This is what your readers want to experience; a transformation. A realisation. A growth. A real, compelling reason for them to stick with the character right to the end. They want to believe that the character can overcome their flaws in order to succeed. They want to see the character become a better person somehow. They want to know that it is possible for a person to change.

When you're writing about dystopian and post-apocalyptic futures, everything is about change.

It is about characters learning to live with the after effects of those changes, both with the physical landscape, and the social, political one. It is about people settling into a new world order, whether they accept and adopt the new set of rules, or whether they fight against them.

Beyond the characters, the world itself is changing. An apocalyptic event will transform the planet itself. It might change the climate, or even the makeup of the atmosphere. It might change the layout of oceans and land. It might turn mountains into valleys, deserts into lakes, and transform the icy poles into dusty wastelands. It may, even, see the planet destroyed altogether.

In a dystopian future, society may have changed beyond recognition. That change may have been triggered by an apocalyptic event, and so, there may be the same physical changes to the planet itself to deal with. But, nothing is forever, and, perhaps, every empire is destined to fall.

These new worlds, despite all of the changes they have undertaken so far, are not done yet. Not if your characters have anything to do with it.

While your characters have their own journeys to travel, and things to learn about themselves, they will also be striving to tackle the world they find themselves in.

Your book, or series, may take place over just a few days or weeks, all the way up to several centuries. No matter how much time your actual book covers, there was change that led to that point, and there will be change that happens after. It's your job to show how much changes during this time. And how much your characters change it. And exactly how they make that change happen.

Just as heroic acts can be both huge, monumental, earth-shattering acts, as well as tiny, personal, even everyday ones, so too can change. Change can be brought about at the tip of a sword or the barrel of a gun. It can be violent, and bloody, and screamed out by a million people. But it can also be the shock of a single event, with the tide of support slowly shifting. It can be a change of heart, or a reassessment of goals. It can be revolutionary, or diplomatic. It can be instantaneous, or it can be gradual.

But, one thing it should be in your story, is hard won. It should take sacrifice, and struggle, and failure. It should involve tough decisions, with your characters needing to make the hardest choices, and give up things that they value and love. It should push your characters to their very limits, testing them, and almost breaking them. And it should, most certainly, change them forever.

Just as your characters set out to change the world, the world will also change them. Their arcs will be intertwined, tangled, and inseparable.

REVEALING WORLDBUILDING THROUGH CHARACTER

Your world, and your characters, are not separate entities. They impress upon one another all of the time, and in a myriad of ways.

Your character will always be moulded and influenced by someone else's vision. Rules, laws, and cultural expectations are passed down generation to generation. They are also passed down from the ruling class to the subordinate one.

When a new law is passed, who benefits? And in what way do they benefit? Your ruling class—be it a monarchy, a government, or a circle of mages—passes rules that back-up their own view of the world. Their understanding of how it works. Their understanding of what life is like.

This includes their understanding of what day-to-day life is like for people they have never met. Majority groups as well as minority ones. Possibly people who speak a different language to them, people who have a different cultural or religious background. It includes people of different genders and sexualities. It includes people with different abilities. It includes people with daily struggles and concerns that they, themselves, probably can't even imagine.

As a result, the world that the ruling class create; the culture, the laws, the education system, the welfare system, health, punishment, everything, is based on their single viewpoint. On a viewpoint that cannot, possibly, encompass the daily reality for everyone. A viewpoint that often excludes certain parts of society, whether through active, knowing discrimination or purely through non-inclusion. By the ruling class not understanding them, or not seeing them at all.

Your character's position in the world, and the way in which it impacts their everyday life; their rights, their freedoms, their restrictions and exclusions, moulds who they are, how they view the world, and what their goals are. It also impacts what their barriers and conflicts are for achieving their goal.

As your character walks around in their world, and interacts with it, they can reveal the worldbuilding. Through their own eyes. Through their physical interactions, their thoughts, and their emotions. The very best way to reveal your worldbuilding to your readers, is through your character's eyes.

Rather than explaining your world through narrative, through info-dumping, it's far better to show it through your character. A good way, is letting your character describe the world they see. A better way, is having your character talk about the world with others. The best way, is to have them actively interact with and react to the world.

You can show that the most bizarre things are completely normal in that world by having the character not react to it at all. To accept it with a shrug. You can highlight cultural points by how your character feels about them, especially if they're breaking social norms, and rebelling. You can create inner conflict, have them struggle with decisions, and have those deeply ingrained cultural rules stop them from pursuing their goal. At least, for a while.

Language is also a really good way to reveal worldbuilding. What sayings are common in your world? Which differ from the sayings we're used to hearing around us? Are there things that they say that are shocking and taboo?

Think about the slang words your character uses, and which are specific to your world. Consider where those slang words have originated from. The media? Another culture? An event? Is it a buzzword created by the government themselves? Consider the impact and the intention of those words. Are they designed to exclude and degrade a particular demographic? Are they twisted from their original meaning? Have they been adopted by the group they were used against, and turned around to be used as a word of power? Consider the reactions that happen when these words are used, and by whom. Some characters may get away with using them, while others can't.

In the same way, what swear words are used in your world? Who do people swear to, pray to, and blaspheme? Do they say "Oh, my God" or something else?

Also look at what they tell jokes about. And who they tell jokes about. What do they find funny? Of course, humour is often used as a defence mechanism, and satire can be used to either highlight a sore point in society, or to give people a moment of comic relief. Perhaps it's used to belittle and make fun of the problem, so that, finally, it doesn't seem so monstrous and insurmountable.

Consider subjects that are shied from, and those that are banned altogether. Do your characters enjoy a certain amount of freedom of speech, or are they constantly fearful of arrest should they speak out of turn? Do they have whispered conversations behind their hands? Do they speak in code? Who is watching, who is listening, and how are they doing it? Think about the punishments for people who speak out against the establishment. Perhaps they simply disappear, and no one ever knows what happened to them. Maybe they are publicly punished as a warning to others.

You can reveal worldbuilding through practically every aspect of your character's life, and you can reveal more about your character by exploring how they feel about it. Whether or not they rebel.

What does an average day look like in their life? Do they go to school, to work? Do they remain at home in a domestic role? Who are they mixing with, or are different sections of society kept separate? Perhaps their job requires them to be around people with totally different lives. Maybe they work for wealthy people. Are they envious? Resentful? Or does it encourage them to work harder, to be ambitious? What are the chances they have to improve their own situation?

How regulated is their life, and their role in it? Does social mobility exist, or are their lives set from birth? Consider how these things differ for different groups in your society. Gender, sexuality, race, religion, ability, skin colour, socio economic status. Consider the things that people can change about themselves, and the things they can't change. Within that, think about the things society *thinks* they can or can't change, or the things that can change for them from an outside influence.

Every aspect of your character, and their life, is influenced by the world in which they live. They can either accept that influence, and be ruled by it, or they can stand up and fight back. In whatever way they are able.

REVEALING WORLDBUILDING THROUGH STORY

In the same way that you can reveal your worldbuilding through your character, tying the two together, you can also reveal it through story. Your world should be created in such a way that your story could only happen there. Likewise, your story should be a perfect fit for your world.

Consider the various settings in which your story takes place, and what they can reveal about your world.

Perhaps your characters have interactions in religious buildings, or at sacred sites. Perhaps they attend official council buildings, or official rites of passage, such as weddings or funerals. Where do people in your world go for their leisure time? What kind of shops are on their high streets? What are the workplaces like, and how do people commute?

Each time your story takes your characters somewhere new, there are chances to reveal more of the worldbuilding. Remember, to fully immerse your readers in your world, you should look to use all of your character's senses. Think about what they can hear, taste, smell, and feel, as well as what they can see. Also consider what they notice first. What jumps out at them as unusual or noteworthy? This can reveal both character and worldbuilding particulars.

There may be big events that happen during your story. An election, the death of a monarch. A war, an annual festival. A census, an anniversary of a historic event. There may be a human sacrifice, a genocide, or the forced evacuation of a populace. There might be a discovery, an invention, or a pandemic. All of these things, and the ways in which your characters react to, carry out, and cope with them, can reveal more about your world and the way it works.

Think about how well-placed your society is to cope with a disaster or unexpected event. Think, also, about who is best-equipped to cope, to survive, and why they are better placed than other people. It might be that the wealthy have their own, personal nuclear bunkers. It might be that they have far better healthcare, and that vaccines are distributed to them first. One demographic of your population might be physically immune to something, or naturally stronger, or more resilient. It might be that, in the case of a famine, the poor are far more resourceful and faster to adapt.

Coming back to a singular level, consider your character's main goal, and their motivations for wanting it. What in your world has inspired them to fight for this thing that they want? Perhaps they are fighting for the freedom to marry who they love, rather than who is prescribed to them. Maybe they are striving to reach a safe haven many, many miles away. One that they aren't even certain exists. Whatever their goal is, how have the particulars of your world brought about this desire in them?

Whatever their goal, you must put barriers in their way. It must be difficult for them to achieve, whether physically, emotionally, morally, or by literally coming up against someone who's determined to see them fail. This is what creates conflict in your story, and without it, you simply don't have a story at all.

Sometimes though, the main antagonist of your story isn't a human adversary. Sometimes, the antagonist is the government, the society, the laws and rules, or the actual, physical landscape of the world.

When crossing a post-apocalyptic wasteland to find sanctuary, your character may encounter other people who seek to stop them. They might run across slave traders, muggers, murderers. They might come across people needing their help, which takes them off the course of reaching their goal. But it may be the last few miles of their journey, maybe a perilous climb across a snow-covered mountain range, that proves to be the barrier that almost sees them fail entirely.

All of these things reveal more about your world; about the setup of society, about the infrastructure and the leadership. And about the physical landscape itself.

USING YOUR WORLD AS A SOURCE OF CONFLICT

Let's dig a little deeper into using your world as a source of conflict in your story. Conflict is a vital component of any story. It adds tension, excitement, a sense of danger: it is the wondering whether, or not, your character will achieve their goal, and how they will do it, that keeps your readers hooked. Without barriers, without try/fail cycles, your character will achieve their goal on the first page, and your story finishes there.

Dystopian and post-apocalyptic worlds are perfect for creating barriers and challenges for your characters. And it's not just because they are awful, difficult, unfair, undesirable, sometimes deadly places, filled with equally awful, difficult, unfair, undesirable, sometimes deadly people. It's because, if the world itself stands in the way of your character, they have two choices. They either give up on their goal, or they change the world itself.

As I've said before, dystopian and post-apocalyptic worlds are all about change. Place your character in an unliveable, insufferable situation, and they can either let it beat them, or they can stand against it. And challenge it. And change it.

But first, they have those pesky barriers to overcome.

Person vs Nature:

Your characters may need to navigate forests, deserts, mountains, oceans, wastelands. How can your characters cross them? How can your characters survive while they are there? Consider what survival skills your characters might have. Think about which of their natural traits might help or hinder them.

What about the atmosphere? Is it breathable? Do they need to shelter from deadly rain, or wind, or other weather phenomena? What else out there is dangerous? What else is trying to kill them?

Consider what your characters already have on their person, and how much they can actually carry. What resources can they use from the landscape around them? What food can they forage for, trap, or hunt? Do they know the difference between food that is safe to eat, and food that is poisonous?

Person vs Authority:

When simple day-to-day survival is difficult, when it's an exhausting struggle, it's hard for your characters to find the time or the motivation to focus on anything else. Especially if that something else is leading a rebellion.

Consider the ways in which the ruling class subdues and crushes the morale of the populace, and their incentive to push for change. Through things like media and advertising, employment, politics, laws, education, religion, healthcare. Consider how they might use things as propaganda. Maybe to convince everyone that things are as good as they can be, or that there are better things to come, if they work hard enough. Perhaps they use removal of such things as a threat to encourage obedience. Maybe to distract them with other, meaningless aspirations. If you can convince people that the latest, far too expensive, piece of technology is the one thing that will improve their lives, they will strive for that, instead of looking for other ways to improve things.

Perhaps the ruling class sets up a certain demographic of society as scapegoats. Convincing everyone that their problems are caused by those people over there, rather than letting the finger of blame fall upon themselves.

If your characters are oppressed, they will need to rise above almost insurmountable barriers such as socio-economic restrictions, freedom of movement, access to education, and a lack of other resources, such as weapons, or meeting places, or communication devices. They may also be closely monitored by heavy surveillance and police presence.

Person vs Laws:

The laws may restrict the ability to travel and move around. Your characters may be restricted on where they can go, or the methods of transport that they have access to. There may be a curfew that they have to adhere to, or a requirement for them to regularly register at a particular location.

There may be check-points that they need to pass through. They may be checked for signs of disease, or paranormal abilities, or they may be stuck in a quarantined area. They may be tracked via facial recognition, or need to pass through gates that require confirmation of fingerprints or retina scans.

It may be that it is illegal for people to gather in large numbers, making it difficult to make plans with other people.

Person vs Society:

Your characters may come up against barriers in the way society organises itself. They may have to fight against gender roles and expectations, or may be too far down the hierarchy to be listened to. They may need to gain access to particular people, and convince them to act as a spokesperson. This access, and their voice, may be hindered by their class, by their age, their colour, religion.

If they're looking to gain support, to 'rally the troops', they will have to fight against apathy and acceptance of the status quo. They will have to fight against the idea that things are already the best that anyone can hope for, or the worry that they might actually make things worse for themselves. Many people will be too fearful of the consequences to join the fight for change.

People, especially those living in dystopian and post-apocalyptic worlds, have their own share of problems to deal with. They are likely to be more concerned with putting food in the bellies of their children than assisting in a rebellion against the state.

When you're putting these barriers in front of your characters, think about how you can raise the stakes further. It may be that their goal focus is interrupted by a new, more urgent goal: the goal to survive, or to escape after being captured, or to rescue someone else who has been captured. Consider, perhaps, things that your character might do to try and improve their situation, that actually end up making it worse.

CREATING FUTURE WORLDS: SOCIETY

When you're considering how to construct your vision of the future, there are a few decisions to be made upfront.

- Is your future world a continuation of societal growth, or has there been a huge upset or cataclysmic event?
- If so, did this event send society off on a different path, or has it been forced to completely start over from scratch?
- Where on the timeline is your story taking place? Are you several generations from the event, or has it only just happened?

Let's tackle each of these possibilities in regards to what society looks like.

A Continuation of Societal Growth:

A great way to start out creating your future society, is by looking back to the past. What social changes and shifts have you seen in your own lifetime? How has the political landscape changed, and people's involvement in politics? How have opinions and beliefs shifted? Think about things such as gender, sexuality, gender roles. Think about people's attitudes to race, religion, language.

Look at what people have voted for and petitioned against. Which issues have driven government election campaigns? Which issues have people been most vocal on, and most polarised? Look at who has been standing up and demanding change, and the opposition they have faced.

Also consider the changes that have been strongly opposed by many people, but have been pushed through anyway.

Think about how society differed when your parents were your age. And when your grandparents were. Now, start to imagine how it might be different for your children. Your grandchildren.

Lead your thoughts down that line, following the trends you've already seen coming through from the past. How might things change for the better? How might they change for the worse? Look at which demographics of society will be the winners and the losers.

Of course, you may come up with an idea for a future society and backwards engineer it instead. While it can be helpful to understand how society grew from today's world to your future vision, it's not essential that you work out every tiny detail.

Your understanding of every moment in the history of your world does not need to be infallible and exhaustive. Especially if it prevents you from simply creating a really cool and exciting future world.

A Cataclysmic Event Derailing Society:

When an unexpected, unprecedented event happens, something mankind has never dealt with before, it can change everything. It can leave society reeling, and desperately looking for solid ground.

If you're taking this approach, you have more free reign in the development of your society. However, there are still important considerations to bear in mind.

This is where you need to fall back on that old adage 'write what you know'. It is one of the most quoted writing tips, and one of the most misunderstood. Writing what you know does not mean that you are restricted to only writing within the scope of your own experience and knowledge. It does not mean you can't write about dragons, or monsters, or multiple vengeful gods. It doesn't mean you can't rewrite history, and it doesn't mean you can't imagine the future.

Writing what you know means that you should bring your own experience and knowledge to the table, not that you are confined by it.

Believe me, your readers will have no issues with suspending their disbelief if you want to write about fantastical, magical, or monstrous things. They will accept the inclusion of aliens, or zombies, or mind-reading. What they will struggle with is you depicting people, and their behaviour, in a way that makes no sense. In a way that goes against their nature. In a way that doesn't mesh with what we all know about the way humans are.

You can derail society in any way you see fit. You can turn society on its head. You can push your characters into completely unknown situations. But, one thing will always be true: they are still human, and they will act as humans act.

Of course, you have the whole scope of human personalities to play with. But think about the traits you know to be true. Such as those in power wanting to stay in power. Such as people being (often unintentionally) selfish, or things like herd mentality, or people clinging together and seeking out sanctuary with others. While some people will exploit the opportunity of a societal breakdown, most will retain their humanity. They'll look for leadership, and structure, and rules. They won't want chaos, and they won't want to make decisions for themselves.

Take what you know about people, and the ways in which society is structured, and start there. You don't need to take society down the most obvious, likely, or logical route, but you need to make your characters believable in the way they react to everything that happens around them.

Society Starting from Scratch:

You may have an event happening that entirely wipes out life as we know it. Perhaps millions, or billions of people are killed. Perhaps the land disappears under water, or ice, or fire. Maybe humans are forced to settle on another planet, or they are left homeless, floating listlessly through space.

As the author (for the little authority that actually grants you), you will need to build a new society, creating it from the tatters and rags that are left. Again, it's time to return to writing what you know.

Think about who the responsibility of leadership falls to, or who steps forward and snatches it. The strongest person? The loudest? The most violent? Who feels they deserve it, that it is their right? Perhaps someone is democratically elected by the remaining people. Humans like leadership. They like ritual, routine, and structure. Whether officially or unofficially, and whether it is the will of the populace or not, someone, or a group of someones, will have to take charge.

There will be followers, and there will be leaders. What happens if a reluctant leader is forced to step up? What happens if an inappropriate leader is chosen? What happens if two leaders claim power, and the new society becomes segregated?

Maybe your new society will seek to structure itself entirely differently to what came before. Perhaps they seek to right some wrongs by forging a new path. Does it work? Can it work? Give 200 people an equal voice, and you may have 200 different ideas of how things should be done.

Timeline Differences:

If you're setting your story straight after, or during the time that everything changes, you'll be depicting the world in a state of panic and disarray. There will be no structure, no 'normal', no hierarchy.

There will be lawlessness, and desperate choices being made. You may choose to base your story around the rebuilding of society. The power struggles, the decisions, the enforcement of the new norm.

You may, however, choose to set your story further along the timeline. Several generations, or even centuries after the event. By this time, society will have found a new balance, however teetering and tottering it might be.

A new hierarchy will have settled, a new governance with laws, rules, and specific roles for everyone. It may be very similar to the society you live in now, or it may be very, very different.

Whatever approach you choose for your book, wherever you place it along the timeline of change, keep thinking back to what you know. Keep a focus on what makes humans humans. And what they act like when they're in groups. Think about the things they strive for, the things they want their society to be. Just as each individual character has its own set of goals and motivations, so too does society as a whole.

It may seek to rebuild the world as it used to be. It may seek to restore communication and technology. It may want to live peacefully alongside nature, rather than trying to dominate and control it. Your society might want to take over everything, to invade and conquer.

Bring the structure of your society back to its goals. What does your society value and treasure? Which people are respected and revered? The way it acts within itself will be tied to those goals.

And, of course, you have to ask yourself: whose goals are they? And who is set to benefit most?

CREATING FUTURE WORLDS: INEQUALITY

When you're creating a dystopian world, inequality is a key feature. It may not, necessarily, be inequality based on wealth. Within any society, you have many, many different demographics of people. They can be grouped by things such as gender, religion, ethnicity, age, or they can be grouped by whether they prefer Star Wars or Star Trek, or if they like pineapple on pizza.

In your dystopian future, you can choose to exclude or oppress any of these groups of people. You could outlaw reading, or ban cheese. You could prevent pregnant women from using public transport, or only provide healthcare to Christians. You can make it as grossly unfair, or petty, or inexcusable as you wish.

However, you need to think about how this law has been passed, and how it has been accepted in society.

Throughout history there are countless examples of laws being passed that oppressed or excluded one demographic or another. There have been laws that allowed them to be treated like animals, or owned like property, or killed in their millions. They may be things that we gasp at, shaking our heads and muttering "it could never happen today". But, guess what? It can happen, and it is happening, right now. Even in the culture you're currently living in.

Look around you. Really see other people. Look at how different groups are treated by the media. Look at how those portrayals bleed out into the consciousness of society, and how they are reflected in politics.

Who are the scapegoats? What language is used to dehumanise them? If you can convince the majority that this particular minority group are the cause of all the country's problems, then you can start dehumanising them. You can call them rats, leeches, or cockroaches. Once you dehumanise them, people won't care what happens to them. They won't care how they're treated, how they're marginalised and, finally, excluded altogether. Because, the country will be better off without them. Because they're rodents, pests. Right?

With the right campaigns, and the right language, and a gradual nudging, it can be quite terrifying the things that society will accept. And support. And actively do.

So, when you're creating your inequality, think about how it has been pushed through. Starting out with little, seemingly harmless things that benefited the majority. It was for the greater good. The lesser of two evils. And, as the majority benefits, they are more willing to accept the next steps, and the bigger steps, all the way up to the inhumane, even murderous ones.

Of course, change could have been pushed through by brute force. By a militarised approach to enforcement. As long as it's someone else being attacked, you can slip away unnoticed. And the fear of being in their place, of the attention suddenly falling on you, well, it makes it easier to look the other way. To not see. With the right 'incentives', a forceful ruling class could push through just about any change they wanted without much opposition. A scary thought.

A lack of power to oppose the government can also be brought about by incremental changes to the voting system. Quietly. Done under the radar. Change the length of term for a government. Remove powers for the courts to oppose them. Shift some of the voting constituency borders to ensure a victory. Slowly, slowly, gently, gently. Until you have a dictatorship, and hardly anyone even noticed, let alone opposed it.

Distraction. Misinformation. Propaganda. Dehumanisation. It's scarily simple. And frighteningly effective.

But, of course, you have something your ruling class weren't expecting. You have a hero, and they're just about to rise up from the rubble.

CREATING FUTURE WORLDS: OPPRESSIVE GOVERNMENTS

Another common feature of dystopian futures are oppressive governments. I've already talked a little about how governments might cause, perpetuate, and enforce inequality in society. Let's look a little further into *why* they might do that, as well as various ways in which they might oppress their people.

A government may wish to divide and segregate a society to maintain control over them. If the people were to collude and conspire, if they were to unite, they would become a force strong enough to bring down a government. When different groups become scapegoats, the blame and anger is focussed on them, rather than being focussed on their rulers. Divide and conquer.

There are many other ways a government can benefit from maintaining an unequal society. It may provide cheap, or even free, labour from one or more groups of people. It might allow them to control resources, and the trade and transportation of resources, allowing the beneficiaries to artificially control demand and inflate prices. It might control people through a lack of education, or maintain a population through a lack of healthcare. It might allow a government to control the birthrate, or to claim ownership over a certain demographic of people, their abilities, their traits, even their actual bodies.

An unequal society also gives a government a chance to control aspirations. They might maintain their position by crushing the aspirations of the lower classes, reducing their motivation or energy to rebel. Or it might control their aspirations through the media. If it can control their desire for certain lifestyles, or benefits, or material possessions, it can control their willingness to work hard, with the hope of attaining such things.

The government will put its own interests first; that is, the interests of the ruling class. Of society's richest. If they can exploit something for money, they will. And they will hoard that money, it won't go back into the economy for everyone to benefit. There will be no 'trickle down' effect. The money will only flow in one direction: upwards.

They will be above the law, above investigation, immune from judgement or punishment. They will be judge, jury, and executioner themselves.

You can put your government anywhere you like along the scale of corruption. They may be rather convert in their actions, doing things under the radar, using the gentle nudging technique to slowly, slowly remould the world. They might fully convince much of the population, including society's poorest and most marginalised, that they are working in their best interests. That they can make their lives better, even that they *want* to.

Or, they might be blatantly corrupt, dangerous, and lethal. Their citizens may live in constant terror. Their laws may be rigid and strict, stripping away any kind of individual freedoms. And their punishments may be swift and harsh. The blood on the hands of the government might be dripping from their fingers for all to see.

In a post-apocalyptic world, the rulers may be less of an organised government, and it might differ from place to place. There may be singular, charismatic leaders. There may be violent gangs jostling for control of particular territories. There may be sanctuaries and settlements where everyone gets an equal vote. It depends how long ago the apocalyptic event occurred, and how much society has managed to rebuild and organise itself since.

Perhaps a new government has taken charge. Perhaps people are still looking around for someone to tell them what to do. It's up to you who's going to step up and take charge, and just what kind of leader they might be.

CREATING FUTURE WORLDS: GENERATIONAL CONFLICT

Your world has changed. It has changed from the world we know now, to the future that you have envisioned. Whether that change was gradual, or sudden, it has created a divide. A divide between those who remember the past, and those who do not.

It may be that you no longer have any characters at all who actually remember what life was like before, but you can still have characters who seek knowledge of it. Characters who hoard trinkets from the past, who read the history books, who wish they had been alive to see it for themselves. Those, even, who wish to restore the world to what it was.

Relics of the previous times may be illegal. They may be sought out and destroyed. They may be branded as blasphemy, as heresy, as propaganda and lies. People caught discussing the past may be arrested and punished. There may be a very, very good reason that those in charge don't want people to know what life was like before. What it was like before they were in charge. Maybe, when life was better.

Using two generations, separated by their memories, or lack thereof, of how the world used to be, is a fantastic tool for highlighting the differences. Of contrasting the before and the after.

Their reactions to various aspects of society will be different, with the younger generation blindly accepting the norms that they've grown up with. They may barely question, or even notice things that make the older generation furious or depressed.

They're likely to have different hopes for their society. Some of the older generation might want a return to how things were. They might long for the past, remembering it with romantic notions. Alternatively, they might fear a return to how things were. They might actually prefer the world they live in now, warning their children not to seek out information about the world before.

There is likely to be conflict between the views of the two generations. They're likely to strive for different things, be angered by different things, view different things as unfair. Their idea of what counts as 'lucky' or being 'better off' will differ. And it's probable that they'll have difficulty in empathising with the other's point of view.

We see this lack of understanding between every generation living in the world today. Each generation has lived with different challenges facing them, and we seem to be unable to understand or sympathize with those differing issues and hurdles. We prefer to lay blame, and to play the game of 'who had it worse'. The nicknames of each generation have become insults as much as terms of solidarity.

All of this is a really useful, active, and character-driven way of revealing your worldbuilding to your readers. Showing your world through the eyes of your characters, through their emotions, their words, and their actions, is the best way to do it. It engages your readers, and it deepens their understanding of both the world and the characters simultaneously. These two things become tied together, and your world is, suddenly, much more than a bit of scenery. Actively showing your worldbuilding through your characters is what you should strive for, it's how to keep your readers immersed in your story.

Of course, there's no rule to say that everything before the change was fantastic, and everything after was awful. Your new world might have huge benefits. There may be a cure for cancer. A lack of technology and industry may have cleaned up the atmosphere. A smaller human population might have brought far-reaching benefits to the whole planet. However, that smaller population might be subject to strict sanctions. They might be owned, and branded, like cattle. Women might be sold for breeding.

Consider the different reactions people will have to different aspects of your world. What do they struggle to accept? What do they struggle to physically, emotionally, mentally deal with? Think about all the things that have changed for them, and how the changes might have affected their lives, and the lives of their children and grandchildren. Also, consider what aspirations they might have for the future generations, as well as what they want for themselves.

No society is ever all good. No society is ever all bad. There are winners and losers. There are compromises and sacrifices. In the most awful, desperate, and hopeless of situations, there is always something good to be found. Even if it's just the slightest flicker of hope that things could be better.

CREATING FUTURE WORLDS: TECHNOLOGY

Once again, when you're looking to create something for your future world, the best place to look, is back to the past.

What technological changes, trends, and inventions have you seen in your lifetime? And what does the preoccupation tend to be?

In pretty much every area of technology, we've watched things become more portable, and become smaller, slimmer, more discreet. Computers have evolved from being an entire room of humming towers, to being a slimline phone in your pocket. Medicine has adopted keyhole surgery, with medical implants and devices becoming smaller and smaller.

It's interesting the way in which, as technology has become smaller, more portable, and more personal, it has caused some of it to become less intrusive, and some of it to become moreso.

We're also developing more technology that automates tasks. And technology that we don't even need to touch. From the first remote control television, to voice commands able to turn lights on and off, open and close curtains, and even set the coffee brewing. Sometimes, we don't even need to be close to our devices. We can turn our heating on before we leave the office, we can start the washing machine remotely. We don't even need to find our car keys anymore.

Think about the technology you find most useful. The technology you'd happily see more of. Think about the place it holds in your life, and the influence it holds over your life. Think about how you feel when you don't have it with you. Think about what tasks you'd struggle with, or what things you'd miss, if that technology suddenly disappeared.

Just as with everything else in your future, technology is an evolution. Push the trends you see happening now, and see where they could, potentially, end up. Push them to the extreme limits. See what effect that has on your world, and the people living in it.

Technology is ever more present in our day-to-day lives. It brings improvements, as well as obstructions. It's important, also, to look at people's attitudes towards technology. For some, the ever-presence of the internet has reduced human face-to-face interaction. For others, the internet has allowed them to become friends with people that they would never have met otherwise. It is a lifeline for some, and a serious catastrophe for the mental health of others.

When you're considering the technology that might exist in your world, you need to remember to keep coming back to the characters. How does it impact them? How do they feel about it? What conflict does it bring?

Also, think about the difference between the technology people *choose* to use, and that which is *enforced* upon them.

Technology has had a huge impact on people's privacy. It is incredibly difficult to leave no digital footprint at all. Many people have been uneasy about the increase in surveillance technology. For others, it has made them feel safer. Our faces are automatically recognised, our car number plates automatically read. Our locations are tracked. We have devices in our homes that are constantly listening. How far does this technology have to go before *everyone* starts to feel uneasy? Is there even a tipping point at all?

In a dystopian world, think about how the ruling class might use this technology as a means of control, oppression, and enforcement. Think, also, about the disparity between the different demographics of your society. Who has access to the technology? Who is excluded from it? How? Why? Who can afford it? Who does it benefit? Does everyone want it?

Let's consider the question of consent. In the world today, consent is a hot topic in regards to technology. Children aren't always allowed access to social media, and aren't always able to legally give privacy consent. Meanwhile, their parents are plastering photos of them online, way before they are able to physically voice their objections, and way before they're able to understand the issue of consent. But, they're caught on surveillance cameras every day. They're marketed to, their use of the internet is tracked, and stored. Just how real is consent? Or are we simply offered enough of it that we're fooled into feeling like we're in control? Have you ever read the privacy notice of a website before using it?

How might consent work in your future world? Perhaps babies are implanted with trackers, maybe DNA is extracted at birth and stored on file. Who gives consent for this to happen? Do the parents have a choice, or is it enforced by law?

Look at how technology has been integrated into all aspects of human life: healthcare, education, law and order, the family. What improvements has it brought? How is it interfering or intruding?

It may be, however, that your future world doesn't represent a continuing evolution of technology. In the case of a post-apocalyptic future, technology may no longer exist at all. You might be creating a scavenger future, where people pick through the useless carcasses of obsolete technology to create new things. Things that work by crank, or by steam.

Perhaps the removal of technology has been a purposeful choice. Perhaps the apocalyptic event was caused by our reliance on technology. A robot uprising.

It might be that technology has been removed from the people. That they abused it, or used it in ways that challenged the authorities. Or maybe they have rejected it because the authorities were using it to spy on them, to control them.

Remember that a technologically advanced society isn't necessarily a more advanced one. Likewise, a society that has regressed technologically, isn't necessarily a less advanced one.

The loss of technology could be beneficial to the citizens. It could be beneficial in some ways, but harmful in others. Or it could be beneficial to some people, but not others.

How do your characters cope with the loss of the internet? With the loss of long-distance communication? Cars, heating, toasters. How would you cope?

CLIMATE CHANGE: SOLARPUNK AND CLI-FI

Despite the deniers, climate change is becoming an increasingly debated topic at the forefront of politics. It is still a polarising topic, based on complicated calculations, and educated guesses, and theories supported by science which is well beyond the grasp of the average person.

Of course, the world has existed for billions of years, and has been through many changes in that time. Humans have existed for a tiny fraction of its lifetime. It's just a shame that we seem to think we own this planet, rather than realising that we are simply borrowing it for a little while.

Whatever your position in the climate change debate, one thing is for certain: we live on a planet with limited space and finite resources. Living as sustainably as we can is beneficial to us, every other living creature, and the planet itself. Sustainable living gives all of us the best chance of long-term survival.

While genre terms such as 'solarpunk' and 'cli-fi' are incredibly recent additions to the ever increasing list of subgenres, it is expected that their popularity will grow.

When I was a child, very few people recycled. It was considered a rather 'hippy', alternative thing to do. Now, it's the complete norm. Even my preschooler knows what can be recycled and what can't. Climate change, recycling, sustainable living. It is becoming one of the most debated topics across all of the generations. People are interested, businesses advertise their green credentials, new laws are changing the attitudes and everyday behaviour of people. I feel a genuine wave of guilt and judgement if I'm ever caught in a shop without my own reusable shopping bag.

Cli-Fi, obviously a contraction of the term 'climate fiction', is a very new term, but the concept has appeared in books for much, much longer. Jules Verne wrote about climate change in his 1889 novel *The Purchase of the North Pole*, in which the climate is affected due to tilting of the earth's axis.

While Cli-Fi can take place in the world we're living in today, it is often a future imagining, and regularly seen in dystopian and post-apocalyptic stories. It's a great angle to explore, and one that offers an entire spectrum of possibilities. Whether you take it somewhere dark, desperate, and filled with death, or whether you take it somewhere hopeful and upbeat, where humans live peacefully alongside nature, is completely up to you.

Solarpunk is another subgenre term which has cropped up recently, encompassing not just literature, but a whole range of mediums such as art, fashion, and music. Its aesthetic uses lots of highly ornamental nature motifs, drawing inspiration from Art Nouveau, and rebelling against clean, modern aesthetics.

Solarpunk focusses on sustainable living, renewable energy, social equality, and a positive outcome for humans and the natural environment. It is a hopeful, often utopian imagining of the world, but one that you can still tie into your dystopian or post-apocalyptic future. Perhaps your characters seek to transform your world into a solarpunk utopia. Maybe an apocalyptic event decimates the human population, and allows the survivors to start over, this time in harmony with the environment. Or, perhaps, your solarpunk utopian society has an underlying shadow of corruption: a dystopian world in disguise as something perfect.

There are many more '-punk' subgenre terms that are emerging now, such as **ecopunk** which focus on the interaction of people with their environment, although it isn't necessarily a post-climate change one, or a sustainable living one. It simply brings together the terms 'ecology', meaning the study of the relations of organisms to one another and to their physical surroundings, and the term 'punk' which, in this context, refers to ideas of the frustration of the working class and young generation, and anti-establishment attitudes

It's quite similar in focus to **salvagepunk**, in that both bring to the fore the intricacies of the supply chain, the manufacturing process, and the sourcing of materials. They focus on where objects actually come from, who designed them, who made them, and, even, who transported them. They seek to highlight the re-usability of materials, the innovation of recycling, and the romanticism of the 'make-do and mend' model.

They can also be seen as genres that shine a spotlight on entrepreneurship, small businesses, and shopping locally. Whether that is through choice, or necessity of circumstance.

Either way, these are all subgenres with a lot of scope to fit into your book, whether you title them as such, or not. There's a lot of fun to be had with these ideas, and you can borrow elements, mash them together, and see what comes out. Perhaps you could even create a new -punk subgenre of your own!

A CHANCE OF REDEMPTION

A dystopian world is, by its very definition, a pretty tough, dismal place to live. Post-apocalyptic worlds aren't exactly an ideal vacation either.

Both worlds require your characters to toughen up in order to survive. They'll offer up some hard, maybe deadly, lessons, and your characters better learn fast if they want to live.

One way that these kinds of environments test your characters is by giving them some truly difficult decisions. Your characters may find themselves choosing between two equally awful outcomes. Making sacrifices. Trying to figure out the lesser of two evils. They may need to act completely against their nature, and their moral code.

Your characters may find themselves with little choice but to steal from the dead, or to abandon a sick or injured friend along the way. They may even need to kill someone in order to survive themselves. But this doesn't mean they become the villain, or that they're even an anti-hero. You can have your hero carry out some terrible acts without losing the sympathy of your readers.

The important thing is to give weight to those choices, and clearly communicate your hero's internal struggle. This doesn't mean that, every time they have a hard decision to make, you drop into a four page internal monologue in which they argue with themselves for hours. We'll leave that to Shakespeare.

There are far more active ways that you can show them weighing up the decision without losing your reader's interest, or slowing the story down. You can show them hesitating, or trying to pass the decision on to someone else. You can have them make the wrong, but kinder, choice several times, and suffering for it, before they finally rise up to make the right, but harsh, decision.

After the choice has been made, your hero might punish themselves, or seek out some kind of forgiveness. They might spend a long time justifying the decision, or find a way to make amends, and rebalance their karma.

You can also give them consequences for their choice, and let them graciously accept the penalty, feeling that it is entirely deserved.

Your hero can still be a truly good person, even when backed into a corner with no other way out.

When you're facing your characters with choices, always bring it back to their motivations. Their ultimate goal. Think about how the decisions play into that, either to derail their quest, or to help them along the way.

What's more important; doing something bad to get them closer to their goal, or doing something good that moves their goal further away, or removes it completely? Which choice will cause more long-term hurt? Their goal isn't always just something for them, it might be a goal to save all of humanity. That's not something they would give up on lightly.

And, it's not just your characters that might need to have a chance at redeeming themselves. Your world itself has become a cruel, unfair place, and there needs to be a chance that it can change. That things can be turned around, reversed, set right. Maybe, even, forgiven.

REVOLUTION, RETRIBUTION, RESOLUTION

Dystopian and post-apocalyptic worlds are worlds of change. We see characters forced to accept, and learn to live in, a whole new environment. Be that a new order to society, or a changed physical landscape. We see characters adapting, learning. And we see characters seeking change, rising up, making their world a better place.

Your ending may come at the end of a single book, or it may be a longer arc that follows through an entire series. However, at some point, you need to resolve all of those story strands; the character arcs, and the arc of the world itself.

Your readers have come along with you on the journey. If you've done your job right, they've loved your characters enough to cry with them, to feel their fear, and to truly, truly want to see them win. Throughout your book, you've promised your readers things. By setting up your genre, and using the tropes your readers recognise, by foreshadowing the things that are going to happen, and by following a solid story structure, you have created reader expectations. Promised them that, if they continue reading, they will have each of those expectations satisfied. You have raised questions that they want to see answered. It may not be in a way that they expect, it may, even, pull the rug out from under them entirely, but it should satisfy them nonetheless.

The revolution is the climax of your story. It is the turning point, where good stands against evil. It is the moment when your hero can win, or when they can lose everything.

Your revolution does not need to be a revolution in the classic sense. It doesn't necessarily fit your story, or your characters, to see them leading an uprising of the people. An army of the oppressed. It may be your character revolting against the harsh, new landscape. Or, it may be a personal revolt against who they used to be. A revolt against the traits that have been holding them back.

Your revolution is yet another moment of change. Change for your world, change for your character. It is the moment when what was transitions into what will be. However, there are still accounts to be settled. A debt must be paid. For the change to happen, for the new to be welcomed in, sacrifices need to be made by the losing side. Perhaps, also, the winning side.

It might mean the assassination of a corrupt leader, the government relinquishing control to the rebels. It may require a public admission of guilt, and state secrets, the release of prisoners, or the handing over of rulers to be tried in court.

It might mean your hero sacrificing something personal to get a better deal for society. Perhaps your character needs to, finally, give up something they've been clinging onto if they want to see the victory through. Maybe they need to hand the power and control to someone else, or let someone else take the credit.

After the debt is paid, your world, your characters, can finally settle into a state of resolution. They can find their new norm. This may see them looking at a rebuilding of society from scratch. It may be a return to the way things were before. It might be a new relationship between humankind and nature. Perhaps the discovery of a new planet able to sustain human life.

You might choose to show your new world, your post-revolution world, and introduce your readers to a vision of the improvements that climax brought about. Or, you might decide to stand your characters right on the precipice, just about to jump into whatever lies in wait for them. Hopeful of a better world.

When your characters have been striving for an improved situation, a superior future, your readers need, at the very least, a glimpse of that. A hope that things can, and will, improve.

That's what the journey has been about. That's what you promised. How will you resolve it?

A WORD ON INFO DUMPING AND LEARNING CURVES

Once you have finished building your world, and you are ready to start writing your book, you need to consider how, and how much, of the background information to include.

Don't think that you will be including every ounce of what you've worked on. You won't. You shouldn't. I know, I know, you worked hard on it, but it wasn't wasted, even if it never makes it into your book. It helped you to understand your world, so that you can write about it in an informed, attached, and immersive way. So that you can make it all the more real for your readers.

An 'info dump' is the term used for when a writer pours out information onto the page as if they are writing a history text book. It's dry, it's dull, and, more often than not, it's confusing.

I'm sure you will have heard the old adage 'show don't tell'. This means that you should be *showing* your readers your worldbuilding, through action and dialogue, not simply *telling* them via a historical lecture.

The absolute best way to teach your readers about your world, is through action. This might be your character clashing with police, or it may simply be them navigating the world.

Let me expand on that: if something in your world is absolutely normal, however far removed it is from our world, if you character treats it, and reacts to it, as if it is entirely regular and everyday, then you are teaching your readers about your world through action.

Say, for example, centaurs are a common sight in your world. If your character treats them with no surprise at all, talking to them as if they are another human, then your readers learn that centaurs and humans live alongside one another equally. Or, perhaps your character ridicules, or bullies the centaurs. Or they treat them with respect, or fear. This is what you are teaching your readers about what the norm is in your world. Through action. This is the ideal way to show your worldbuilding.

It's not always so easy.

And so, the next best way is through dialogue. Again, avoid huge blocks of information. This is no different to info dumping, you're simply letting the history lecture come out of a character's mouth. However, they can have a conversation with a friend about a historical aspect of the world, or a cultural aspect. A conversation. Not a lecture.

Sometimes, however, you need to break the rules. I'm not saying that you must *never* simply tell your readers information. Sometimes, it's necessary. Sometimes, it's even the better option. But, do it with careful consideration, and do it sparingly. Rules are, certainly in creative pursuits, meant to be broken.

If you're concerned about whether or not you're getting the balance right, the best way is through the use of beta readers. Beta readers read through early, pre-publication versions of books, and give honest feedback that allows the author to improve their story. If you've got the balance wrong, beta readers can tell you.

Another way to learn this is through reading, reading, and reading. Take careful note of how other authors handle the dilemma. How they get the balance right, and how they get it wrong.

The other way is simply through practice. The more you write, the more you drill down into your personal style and voice, the better you are likely to get at it.

The way in which you give worldbuilding information to your readers also depends on the complexity of your world, and how different it is to ours.

If you're writing about earth, whether in the present, past, or future, there are many things your readers will already know. They understand about time, and seasons. They know the animals, the plants. They know what humans are like, and how they interact. The learning curve of your world may be quite a gentle one.

Everything in your world that is different to our real world, adds to the learning curve of your book. Every mythical creature, every imagined technology, every drop of magic, and every jargon word makes that curve a little bit steeper.

You want to ease your readers in. If, in chapter one, you expect them to learn everything about your world and its history, learn who the characters are, and absorb their struggles and goals, they will be exhausted by the time they get to chapter two.

Tell them what they need to know. They don't need 5 million years worth of military history. They may need flashes of it, but not the entire thing. Be gentle with them. Don't make them do too much work, and don't leave them floundering around your story loaded down with too much knowledge.

Again, these are things that you can learn and improve on with the help of beta readers, by reading, reading, reading, and by simply practising your craft. You will find your way, I promise, but I can't tell you how to do it, because we are all different. And our stories are different. And our voices are different.

You might write short, 50,000 word novels, and leave a lot of the deeper worldbuilding out. You might write 150,000 word epics, with readers who expect a much more immersive experience. Practice, experiment, and you'll find the right balance for you, your books, and your readers.

IDEAS DUMP

As you work your way through this book, you are bound to have flashes of ideas popping into your mind. Character and story ideas, that you're not quite sure what to do with yet.

Don't lose them; those little flashes are important.

Instead, use the following pages as something of an ideas dump. Some of these may never make it into your finished book, but, you never know, you may be able to recycle them into other stories.

No idea is ever wasted…

WANT EVEN MORE WORLDBUILDING?

Our adventures don't have to end here...

You can explore the rest of my series of worldbuilding guides for authors, guiding you through the basics of worldbuilding, helping you to create magic systems and religions, to write dystopian and post-apocalyptic fiction, and to create histories rich with myths and monsters.

Find more information on all of my workbooks and other worldbuilding services at angelinetrevena.co.uk/worldbuilding

Get Your Free Creating a Timeline Worksheet

Join my worldbuilding mailing list to claim your free Creating a Timeline worksheet.

You will also receive all the latest news on releases and workshops, as well as worldbuilding tips, tricks, and resources.

Join at subscribepage.com/worldbuilding

About Angeline Trevena

Angeline Trevena was born and bred in a rural corner of Devon, but now lives among the breweries and canals of central England with her husband, their two sons, and a rather neurotic cat. She is a dystopian urban fantasy and post-apocalyptic author, a podcaster, and events manager.

In 2003 she graduated from Edge Hill University, Lancashire, with a BA Hons Degree in Drama and Writing. During this time she decided that her future lay in writing words rather than performing them.

Some years ago she worked at an antique auction house and religiously checked every wardrobe that came in to see if Narnia was in the back of it. She's still not given up looking for it.

Find out more at www.angelinetrevena.co.uk

Made in the USA
Las Vegas, NV
03 December 2021

35956635R00057